Mike Yr
intrigue ,

last. He has put his thoughts about God's goodness and kindness into words that will touch your heart regardless of where you are in Christianity. I would encourage you to read every word.

—Charles and Frances Hunter
Authors of *Angels On Assignment*

It has been my joy during the past year to meet Mike and Janet Yrigoyen and their two precious children. It is a privilege to be called their pastor.

The Garden and the Word is an inspiring and uplifting work of the Holy Spirit that I can wholeheartedly recommend to any reader. It is a confirmation that God continues to speak to His people and that His present day communication is always in complete harmony with Scripture.

Not only can I heartily recommend this book, but I am delighted that I can also recommend Mike Yrigoyen to you as an authentic person and disciple of Jesus Christ!

—Pastor Terry K. Burchyett
Calvary Christian Fellowship
Franklin, Tennessee

We are impressed with Mike's sincerity and the authenticity of his experiences with the Lord. He has wisely included abundant Scripture references so you may prove "whether those things are so."

—KEN SCHISLER AND
ANNIE SCHISLER, AUTHOR OF *ANNIE'S VISIONS*
MONTEVIDEO, URUGUAY

The Garden and the Word is interesting reading material. It shows how vividly God gives in-depth knowledge of the Word of God to the person who is dedicated to His work.

—PASTOR VARKEY VARGHESE
LIGHT OF LIFE CHURCH
QUEENS VILLAGE, NEW YORK

The Garden and the Word reads like an intimate love letter from the Bridegroom, King Jesus, to us, His bride. The prophetic word is meant to encourage the people of God, and these pages ring with encouragement. This is a passionate call to embrace Jesus, to hear His Word in the very depths of our soul, and to allow it to transform us. This book is meant to be read on your knees. But as you do, the Spirit will draw you closer to Jesus than you ever have been before.

—PASTOR STEVE FRY
BELMONT CHURCH
NASHVILLE, TENNESSEE

THE GARDEN
and THE WORD

MIKE YRIGOYEN

CREATION
HOUSE PRESS
A STRANG COMPANY

THE GARDEN AND THE WORD by Mike Yrigoyen
Published by Creation House Press
A Strang Company
600 Rinehart Road
Lake Mary, Florida 32746
www.creationhouse.com

Unless otherwise noted, scripture quotations marked NIV are from the Holy Bible, New International Version. Copyright © 1973, 1978, 1984, International Bible Society. Used by permission.

Cover design by Terry Clifton

Author photograph by Richard Shipp Photography

Library of Congress Control Number: 2003099175
International Standard Book Number: 1-59185-469-5

04 05 06 07 08—987654321
Printed in the United States of America

This book is dedicated to our dear Lord and Savior, Jesus Christ, who gloriously overcame everything in this world through His intimate relationship with the Father—a relationship of complete love and obedience. His life and great love for each one of us clearly shows us how we are to live out our own lives.

ACKNOWLEDGMENTS

Other than allowing me to know Him, the greatest gift our Heavenly Father has given to me has been the wonderful family and friends He has graciously placed in my life. I want to express my gratitude to the Lord and to offer my sincerest thanks and appreciation to:

My loving wife, Janet. I am privileged to be sharing my life with you, and I love you with all of my heart.

My dear children, Lisa and Daniel. You are such a joy in my life, and I love discovering the beauty and character the Lord has placed within you as you each grow and mature in Christ.

My parents, Frank and Nancy, and my brothers, Frank and Gregg. You can never know how much your love means to me or how I would be so much less without you in my life.

My friends and prayer partners, Ray Short, Parker Kurtz, John Duarte, Jeff Lacki, Shelly Laden, Peter Soule, Cindy Avlaquiotes, and Pastor Varkey Varghese. Together we experienced and heard firsthand much of what is written in this book. I praise God for how you have loved my family and me, and for your faithfulness, guidance, support, and many, many prayers—and for your wonderful hearts for the Lord.

The rest of my family and so many others who have so graciously touched my life. I appreciate you more than you can know, and I pray the Lord will bless each one of you with great peace, joy, and a saving knowledge of His love.

The staff at Creation House Press. Thank you for turning these writings into a book for the Lord.

CONTENTS

INTRODUCTION

I believe writing this book was a work of the Holy Spirit. Although it was "the work of one and the same Spirit," (1 Cor. 12:11) the two sections are of different anointings from the Lord. These works reinforce what is provided for us through the Bible and reveal the character and heart of our Living God.

The first working of the Holy Spirit is called "The Garden" and was given over a relatively short period of time. The Lord began to create in me a great passion and tenderness for Jesus as he travailed in the Garden of Gethsemane. I would see paintings of Jesus in prayer in the Garden and my heart would break for our Lord. I would read about these moments in Jesus' life and I would come to tears for our Savior. I began to have thoughts about what happened in the Garden and how Jesus had endured so much for me. When the intensity of these sentiments increased I began writing what the Lord gave me. The words flowed and I felt the very real and near presence of the Holy Spirit. His presence was a great encouragement that spurred me on many times with the confidence that what was being written was from Him. Whenever I did not know what else to write or was not able to figure out how to word what the Lord wanted to say, I would stop and pray and the words would come. "The Garden" speaks of the Father's great love for us, of the Lord Jesus' unyielding obedience to the will of the Father, and of the example given through the unforeseen nature and hidden purposes of the Messiah as He struggled with the cup given Him—even as we, His children, so often struggle with the cup of the lives given to us.

The second working of the Holy Spirit is, I believe, a higher level of revelation compared to "The Garden." "The Word" is a compilation of prophetic words received from the Lord over a five-year period from 1997 through 2002. When the Lord began to speak His words through me He led me to "write in a book all the words I have spoken to you" (Jer. 30:26). For the purpose of this writing, the prophetic words are the thoughts and heart of the Lord spontaneously spoken by the Holy Spirit through a person using his or her voice. These words were tape-recorded and later transcribed and saved. As time passed, the Lord impressed upon me to search through the words and bring together those that were messages to large audiences, spoken in church services, or that were spoken to individuals but were encouraging or guiding messages that apply to all His children. As the words were chosen, the Lord had me search the Bible to gather confirming Scriptures and match them to His words. While the spoken word is often difficult to fully grasp when first heard, we are better able to review for clarity and understanding what the Lord has said when it is transcribed and able to be read. This allows for reflection and greater recognition that He truly is a living God as He speaks into our lives and our circumstances in this present day. The Holy Spirit's presence and the feeling of the Lord's heart and emotions as His word is spoken have often been overwhelming. The Lord has confirmed to me many times that these are indeed His words—from His heart to our hearts—and are for His children to hear.

The words are "book–ended" with scriptures before and after each word because our Lord is unchanging, and what He says today is consistent with and validated by the Holy Bible.

The combining of these two separate works into a single book is also at the guidance of the Holy Spirit. I believe the Lord has prepared these writings and wants them shared with His children. "All of these must be done for the strengthening of the church" (1 Cor. 14:26).

I. THE GARDEN

My children!
I see you in your life,
I see you in this world,
and to you, My children,
this world is as the garden
that when the rain would come
and the sun would shine
you would look upon the flowers,
you would see their beauty,
and they would bring you joy;
you would look upon the tree,
and it would stand tall before you,
you would take shelter under its leaves,
and it would bring you comfort.
But the things of this world, My children,
are temporary.
Return to the flowers,
return after there has been no rain,
and there is no joy, My children;
return to the tree,
and the leaves have fallen,
and the wind has scattered them.
Where is your comfort now, My children?
Know now that I have called you;
I have spoken your name
that you would look upon the eternal,
things that are everlasting,
that you would look and turn

and you would see the mountain,
and the mountain would stand before you
and though the rain would stop,
yet I do not change;
though the wind would come,
yet I do not move.
Let Me be your comfort.
Let Me be your joy.
Seek Me, My children, in all things,
for I am here for you.
I stand before you,
and even now I speak your name;
even now I call you to Me;
even now I give you My joy
and My comfort and My love.
I am here for you, My children.
I am here for you.
Turn away from the world
and turn to Me.
Turn to Me, My children.
Turn to Me.

CHAPTER 1

THE GARDEN

Then Jesus went with his disciples to a place
called Gethsemane.

—MATTHEW 26:36

On reaching the place, he said to them, "Pray
that you will not fall into temptation."

—LUKE 22:40

And he said to them, "Sit here while I go over
there and pray."

—MATTHEW 26:36

He took Peter, James, and John along with
him, and he began to be deeply distressed and
troubled.

—MARK 14:33

Then he said to them, "My soul is overwhelmed
with sorrow to the point of death. Stay here and
keep watch with me." Going a little farther, he
fell with his face to the ground and prayed.

—MATTHEW 26:38–39

"*Abba*, Father," he said, "everything is possible
for you. Take this cup from me. Yet not what I
will, but what you will."

—MARK 14:36

An angel from heaven appeared to him and strengthened him. And being in anguish, he prayed more earnestly, and his sweat was like drops of blood falling to the ground.

—LUKE 22:43–44

Then he returned to his disciples and found them sleeping. "Could you men not keep watch with me for one hour?" he asked Peter. "Watch and pray so that you will not fall into temptation. The spirit is willing, but the body is weak." He went away a second time and prayed, "My Father, if it is not possible for this cup to be taken away unless I drink it, may your will be done." When he came back, he again found them sleeping, because their eyes were heavy. So he left them and went away once more and prayed the third time, saying the same thing.

—MATTHEW 26:40–44

Returning the third time, he said to them, "Are you still sleeping and resting? Enough! The hour has come. Look, the Son of Man is betrayed into the hands of sinners. Rise, let us go! Here comes my betrayer!"

—MARK 14:41–42

Jesus, knowing all that was going to happen to him, went out and asked them, "Who is it you want?"

—JOHN 18:4

Meditating on the word "garden" usually brings to mind pictures of peace and serenity; pictures of the simple beauty of God's creation which far exceed even the most artistic and intricate works of man; pictures of wonders and diversity of life and color standing before a backdrop of floating clouds and unending blue skies; pictures of colorful flowers, of tall, lush trees offering shade and escape from the midday sun; and of living creatures—insects, birds, and animals—all blending together in harmony and perfection to create a world by itself that, even if it was all of creation, is beyond man's comprehension. The garden, where between flowers of sublime beauty, the spider weaves his web, gently tossed by the unseen wind, unnoticed by the scampering squirrel as it hurriedly searches for its next meal under a blanket of newly fallen leaves. The garden, a place of changing seasons; a place of fertile soil rich and cultivated, ready to nurture the seed planted for growth. A place of new beginnings.

For the Christian, for those who believe in and love Jesus as Lord and Savior, the image of the garden brings very different thoughts and emotions. The Garden of Gethsemane is the place our beloved Jesus suffered in the anguish and sorrow of his heart and soul. The Garden is a place where He waited for the words of the prophets, spoken of Him centuries before, to be fulfilled. The place where He waited to hand Himself over to men so blinded and driven by the hatred and lust of Satan that they would brutalize Him and kill Him. The beauty and harmony of the Garden played host to a moment in time unequaled in sorrow and division of man from God since the foundations of the world—and yet it was all according to the plan, the love, and the will of the Father. The suffering, the torment, the separation from the Father that our Savior endured was for all His children so that we would be healed, so we would have peace, so we would spend eternity with our God. The cruelty of Satan and the pride of man were eclipsed in a single act of supreme love by our Creator.

The contrast between the physical beauty of the Garden and the hideous actions of those who seized Jesus to have Him beaten and killed, is enormous. For what Satan meant for evil, God purposed for good. While Satan sought to torture and destroy, God the Father determined to save and to lift up for everlasting life. In the Garden, what was alive was allowed to die, and, according to God's plan, what has risen from the fallen seed is more beautiful, more enduring, more glorious than that which was before. Today the Garden of Gethsemane is what the eye of the beholder or the faith of the believer would have it be. Either a simple and beautiful place with ancient olive trees, clean and neatly manicured grass, beautiful bougainvilleas and a startling view of the old walls of Jerusalem. Or a place of anguish and sorrow where our Savior travailed for His life but forfeited everything for each of us as the will of the Father required. Or still, a place of victory and new life where prophetic words of the Messiah were fulfilled so that all of those who believe, all those who receive Jesus as the Christ and as their Savior, will have eternal life—a place of new birth!

The Garden of Gethsemane is not merely one of these places, it is all of these places and more. The holiness of the ground within the Garden is beyond our understanding. The deep meaning, the suffering, the anguish, of what transpired on that night for our Lord Jesus is beyond our emotional or spiritual capacity to understand or endure. It remains a mystery. It remains a beautiful testimony of the love of Jesus the Son, and of God the Father, as they sacrificed supremely for their creation, for their own children.

As I have lived my life and as the expectations of my youth have been shaped and molded into the reality of who I am today through the many experiences I have had and the people I have known, I am beginning to know that all that is important, all that is true for each of us as we live our lives, is only made meaningful through the love of God. Our greatest joys, our strongest hopes, our sincerest desires are only made complete as we allow Jesus Christ to be our Lord and Savior. We are complete in God alone. Embracing these words, even merely expressing these sentiments in our thoughts, is a tremendous struggle in the mind—a battle for the intellect of man in a world where success is measured by riches accumulated and the degree to which one lives his desired life. Even as the battle for the mind is won for Christ, the ultimate battle continues to be fought in our heart, for until we believe and surrender in the deepest parts of our soul the battle rages on—and is not truly won. For each of us, the battle continues until we breathe our last breath and receive the ultimate freedom found only when we fall into the arms of Jesus and join our Lord for eternity.

There have been times or areas of my life where I felt I was winning this battle, only to see myself for who I really was and to know that I was less than I had thought. There have been other times or areas of my life where I knew I was falling short, where I knew that I could not make it on my own. In times such as these the Lord has always responded to me in His perfect love. The same love that said, "I am willing" (Matt. 8:3) tells me that He continues to love me despite what I have said or how I have acted. The same love that said, "Take my yoke upon you and learn from me, for I am gentle and humble in heart, and you will find rest for your souls" (Matt. 11:29) still speaks to me today encouraging me to seek after Him and to follow Him. Not because of who I am, but because of who He is; not because of how I act or what I do, but because of what He did on the cross to release His unending love. As I turn to the Lord, as I allow Him to search my heart, He has always been with me to encourage me, to correct me, to guide me, and to help me. With more love than I am able to understand, He has shown me the cracks and flaws in my character, gently working to fill them and cover them to shape me into something more than I could ever be by myself. Even if I wanted to fight this battle on my own, I know it is impossible for me to win without the help of our loving Savior who endured all things for me, even death on the cross.

This is one of the mysteries of our God: that He would die for us even knowing us for who we are. Sometimes, it is easier to see how the Lord would love others, but more difficult to think that He would see the evil that is within me, the corrupt character and selfish ambition that often motivate me, and still call me to His side, still freely give His love to me, still desire to use me for His glory, still give of Himself to me for all time. Even so, I hear His voice as He calls me "my son." His love is beyond me— but it is freely and completely given to me. In His love, He became as a man and suffered every temptation and every emotion common to man—and yet He did not sin. In every word He spoke, every action taken, Jesus always sought to do the Father's will, to bring glory to His name. And such was God's love for me, such is the Father's love for us, that Jesus endured the cross. He endured until the words were spoken, "It is finished" (John 19:30). And as it was finished, the hope for life, indeed the only way for life to be lived eternally, was opened for us—if we would only embrace it!

CHAPTER 2

JESUS' GETHSEMANE

It is not a coincidence that the battle fought in the Garden of Gethsemane by our Lord Jesus is also the same battle that each of us fight daily in our own lives. And it is not by chance that this very same battle was originally fought by the first of our kind in yet another garden so very long ago—by Adam in the Garden of Eden. Every day we struggle to know the will of the Father and to submit to Him. Every day we fight to be holy for our Lord and to do His perfect will. Much of our struggle is against our own emotions and desires that are deeply seeded within us for our own fulfillment and preservation. The Lord knows our struggles and how we feel because He fought the same battles and faced the same struggles to carry His cross that we face in trying to carry our own. Still, it is the Lord speaking, "I love you. I am with you. You are my dear one. You are my child." from the depth of His love and the strength of His experience, that enables me to continue trying. His love and presence in my life are faithful and steadfast even when I am not. We can draw upon His love knowing He will never fail us.

The agony suffered by our Lord as He awaited His betrayal in the Garden of Gethsemane is plainly and succinctly recorded in the Bible. Though I have thought about it and though I have tried, I cannot imagine what our Lord endured for me there. How terrible those few short hours must have been for Him. For Jesus, it was a time when He pleaded with His closest friends to watch and pray with Him saying, "My soul is overwhelmed with sorrow to the point of death" (Matt. 26:38). The plots of the Pharisees did not take Jesus by surprise. Jesus knew that if He moved in any direction except towards the cross that He would have been disobedient to the Father, and that without the cross there would not be the resurrection. And because of this, Jesus' will became that of the Father's—"Yet not what I will, but what you will" (Mark 14:36).

The Lord Jesus was the perfect example of how we are to live our lives when our own desires and purposes are not the same as God's. We are to surrender every detail of our lives to God and be obedient to Him—even unto death. There is no hypocrisy in our standing before a loving, all-knowing God and admitting that we want something different for ourselves than what He wants for us. In the Garden, our Lord Jesus also asked for His own desire. He pleaded to be spared the pain and suffering of the cross. Jesus prayed for another way, and yet He experienced the same crushing sorrow and disappointment that we sometimes experience in our own lives—for the most needful and passionate request in the Son's life on this earth, "Abba, Father" (Mark 14:36)—the Father's answer was no. The test, the struggle that rages within us, is to put ourselves aside and do allow the Father's will. We must be willing to live as Christ who, though being God, was obedient to death on the cross so that we might all have life. We must seek unity in purpose with the Lord, unity in spirit, even when our own desires differ. And we must be joyful knowing that His purposes are complete, that His desire is for the ultimate good. Our purpose and goal and desire must be for the Father. What is more fulfilling, more significant in this life than to do the will of the Father? And how my own will conflicts with His! Like Paul, I can feel the struggle within me. The words are not hard to say, "What a wretched creature I am. Who will rescue me?" (Rom. 7:24). Only Jesus, who became a man like me, who persevered in the same struggles, who fought the same battles, and who now reigns supreme in complete victory.

There have been times when I have thought about our Lord Jesus in the Garden, the great sorrow and anguish that He felt, and I have been overwhelmed with emotion. I have seen paintings or created the image in my mind of Jesus in prayer, knowing what was coming, wanting the cross to be over with and behind Him, but also not wanting to have to endure it—not wanting to have to live it all. I have felt sorrow and deep gratitude, knowing that He suffered the cross because of my sin. He suffered and endured as a lamb led to slaughter so that we would all be able to have His love, His guidance, His purpose for our lives in this world and so that we would share in His glory in the next.

I have been in a bookstore and, seeing the cover of a book with Jesus on it in the Garden kneeling against an angel, the angel gently comforting Him, have been brought to tears knowing how our Lord was grieved and anguished, and still he allowed the unthinkable to happen to Him. I have been lost from the teaching of a Sunday school class as the teacher stood before a painting of Jesus in prayer at the rock in Gethsemane, and deep in my spirit I was trying to express appreciation and love for our Lord that are beyond mere words.

I have walked down the worn and ancient path in the actual Gethsemane in Jerusalem, fresh and cool in the morning sunlight, and felt awe and the presence of His Spirit. I have stood in the Garden and looked up to see the walls of Jerusalem, the Golden Gate looming high above and beyond the deep purple of a bougainvillea's flower whose life twisted upward from the root planted within the soil of Gethsemane, and I felt the enormity of time for what had happened in this place in the past, for what I was seeing and living in that moment, and for what will happen in another time when through other people's eyes the glory of the Lord will be seen as the Golden Gate is opened and Messiah Jesus will physically enter Jerusalem again. Our God is a part of each of these moments in time—the same place but over great expanses of time, the same God and this same small, but vastly significant piece of earth.

I have knelt before the rock that history records as the site where the Lord travailed and suffered as He prayed in His last free moments before the cross, and I longed for that cup to have been taken from Him. I wanted to have been there on that night so that I might have helped Him, slipping into my own vanity that somehow I could have spared Him His suffering, that somehow I could have saved Him from the cross that awaited Him. In more rational times I realize that I am only like Peter was as I place myself between Jesus and the will of the Father—"Behind me, Satan" (Matt. 16:23). I also realize that, again like Peter, if I had been in the Garden that terrible night and had the opportunity to intervene for our Lord, that I, too, would have fallen asleep while in prayer and that I, too, would have fled in confusion and fear for my own life just like the other disciples. I can say this with confidence knowing how I live my life today; knowing that when given the opportunity to pray, how often do I turn out the light and settle into my bed covers when my eyes grow heavy with sleep? When given the opportunity to testify for Jesus, how often do I flee or do I quietly hide within myself, my thoughts and faith obscured in silence and a blank face or a sideways glance? How often am I willing, as Jesus was willing, to put my own desires, my own frailty and weaknesses aside, and do the Father's will? It is with despair in my own heart that I can speak of my failures, that I know how often I fall short.

It is Jesus Himself who continues to encourage me, to guide me, to help me so that I might grow in Him—so that I, too, might live for the Father and be only in His will. It is the life of Jesus himself and the agony of the Garden that prove the test of time and have reached into my heart as a living example. He knows what I have gone through, what I am going through, what is still to happen in my life, and yet Jesus loves me, cares for me, strengthens me—and He sits at the right hand of the Father interceding for my well-being, for my healing, and for my faith! He will never abandon me as He was abandoned. He will never betray me as He was betrayed. He will never mock me as He was mocked. He will never strike me as He was struck. The Lord will only work for my good—as I am willing to do His will. As I am willing to be crucified with Him, I will have all things that He desires me to have.

CHAPTER 3

OUR GETHSEMANE

In my life, the Lord has allowed a very ordinary man to know that I, like everyone else, am special in the ever–present and all–knowing eyes of our loving God who makes all things possible—even my own salvation. Truly, He has saved us all. An eternal God stepped into time and walked with us to show His lost creation and dearly beloved children the true character of the Living Lord. He made a way for us to regain what was lost, to hold what could not be grasped, to live and flourish when death and darkness had swallowed us whole. In the Garden, Jesus faced the same struggle that you and I live each day—and He showed us the answer to our own questions: "How are we to live this life?" "Would a God who loves me ask me to sacrifice so much?" "Wouldn't the Lord want me to do this?" "Wouldn't He want me to have these things?" Jesus is the ultimate example of how our own desires, even the deepest longings of our hearts, even what would seem right and good, can be in conflict with the will of the Father. In those times when the struggle rages within us, we must try with all that we have to hear the Lord and to know His will in our lives. And as we hear, our response must be, "Yet not my will, but your will be done" (Luke 22:42).

Our Lord and Savior chose the will of the Father, and it was the love of the Father—even as it carried Him to the cross, even as He endured the pain and suffering from which He could have saved Himself with a single word—and His complete knowledge of what was for the ultimate good that allowed Jesus to cling to His Father's will. Isn't this the measure of His love? Isn't this the fullness of His love for His Father as well as His love for us?

While the Garden is a wonderful example of how Jesus responded in His life, is this not the great challenge that He has placed squarely in front of us? Is this not an affront to us when we live our lives for our own good? If we are to remain true to our Lord, if we are to serve Him in our lives, if we will truly love God, then we must strive to do just as Jesus did. "Be perfect, therefore, as your Heavenly Father is perfect" (Matt. 5:48). There is no skirting the issue, there is no turning away or closing our eyes. To say that we love God, to say that we believe that Jesus is our Savior and that He lives today, to believe that the Bible is the inspired Word of God, says that we must live our lives as Jesus did and that we must do as He says. As Jesus did the Father's will, can we look at ourselves honestly and not see that for each of us it is also His desire that we do the same? Does He not know the anguish and difficulty we face as our own desires struggle and tear against the perfect will of a humble and self-sacrificing God? Does He not know that in every moment we are assaulted with our own desires, our own pride and lusts? And can He truly love us as He asks us to place this aside? Can Jesus truly love us as He asks us to drink of His cup, to pick up our own cross and carry it each day?

As we look at the life of Jesus, can there be any doubt that our Father in heaven would rather we live in His perfect will, that we would be obedient to His commands and to His call upon us, than for anything else we might do or possess? More than the friends or spouse that He would bring us, He would rather we loved Him. More than the riches of this world, He would rather we store up treasures in His kingdom. More than avoiding trials and sorrows, He would rather our love for Him would be unchanging and unwavering as we endure this life—always giving praise to our Father in heaven.

As I look at the life the Lord has given me, I see that much of what I have wanted at different times in my life would not have been for my own good. Anything that takes me away from the Lord, anything that adds to my pride, anything that allows me to think, even in the subtlest of ways, that I am able to complete my life by myself, that I am self-sufficient, is a challenge to my love for the Lord. The things of this world that I want and am able to pursue and win in my own strength are often a great test of my faith and walk with the Lord. Everything I can do on my own becomes a brick in the wall of pride that I build without any effort and, often, without any knowledge that I'm doing it. So great are the effects of success in this world, even within the ministries I have undertaken within the church, upon my own feeling of self-worth and capability that until I have been far from the place I should be, I have not seen how it has kept me from my Lord. I have become offensive to Him because I have become filled with pride; when it comes to what I see as being best for myself, when it comes to what I want to do, I am often not able to show restraint. If I want to do something and can, I often do it without any thought or consideration of the Lord. If I think it is a good thing, then surely it is God's will for me! It's such a small thing and I know how to do it, why should I pray? I can deceive myself easily—it is my nature.

I see the Lord in the Garden, and I see that I am not like Him. I see that He is holy, that He is love, that He is self-sacrificing. I see that Jesus places others before himself, even though He is God, and that He does what is best for His kingdom. In His love, what is for the good of His kingdom still ends up being for my good in my life as well. Even as Jesus endured the Garden and the cross, so I must endure my garden, so I must carry my cross. I know it is the Father's will that I would watch and pray and listen so that I would know His will for my life. I also know that after understanding His will, I must be obedient no matter the perceived cost. In every aspect of our lives, we need to pray for His will to be done. We need to have the humility to see ourselves through the eyes of God rather than as we choose to see ourselves. We need to kneel in repentance and ask to see His face, ask to be in His presence, and we must be obedient and willing to die to ourselves when He asks us to. We must have the restraint to not fill our lives with things that separate us from God—to choose how we spend our time, and to spend it with the Lord. We must have the restraint to give of our finances as the Lord commands rather than spending on ourselves. If something dishonors our Holy Father, we must be willing to make choices that may embarrass us or cause us to not blend in with the crowd or follow what is popular. We must know that it does not matter what we may think or how we may feel. What He thinks and how

He feels is the only thing that matters.

Can any of us imagine what we would be like, what this world would be like, if Jesus had not shown restraint? What if Jesus had succumbed to His own emotions, His own desires, and had used the power and glory that were His since before creation? What if He had called angels into Gethsemane to rescue Him from the cross? How would history be different for us? How would eternity be different for you and me without the gift of His grace? Considering the cost, considering the example, can we back away from the same challenge in our lives? Can we dare to not follow our Jesus to our own cross since He has already shown us the way that we must live? In everything He asks of us, in our greatest trials, in our deepest sorrows, should not our love grow all the deeper? Should not our words always be of praise to the Lord who gives us life?

As I write these words, and perhaps as you read them, how easy it is to answer, *yes!* But as I live my life, as I make my decisions, and as I face my trials and life's difficulties, how is it that my vision becomes so blurred? How is it that I can forget? How is it that I can place myself before the Lord without a second thought? It is because of who we are that we must cherish the Garden. We must cherish what Jesus did for us, knowing that we cannot do it ourselves. We should know such sorrow and love for what Jesus had to endure for us that we become willing to endure a form of the cross in our own lives—as He chooses.

CHAPTER 4

NEVER ALONE

God loves us more than we can know or comprehend. He loves me, and He loves you. Jesus loved us enough to give up His place with the Father to live His life on earth and to endure His time of suffering and death on the cross so that we would not face eternal death. Still, He ascended to heaven and, because of His life, because of the Garden, because of the cross, there is an empty tomb and the King of kings now sits at the right hand of the Father in all glory and majesty. Without the Garden there would not have been the cross, and because of the cross God's grace and forgiveness have been given to us so that even as we miss hearing our Father's will, even as we know God's will and make different choices, or having made the right choice we are unable to do what He asks, "The spirit is willing, but the body is weak" (Mark 14:38), even as we fail and as we sin, we are covered by God's love and grace. "There is no condemnation for those who are in Christ Jesus" (Rom. 8:1). This is the freedom that we have: that even as we must press in to find the Lord, even as we must seek Him with all of our hearts, even as we must be obedient and follow His will in all things, even as we must be holy as He is holy, even with these standards that Jesus exemplified in His life yet seem unattainable in our own—Jesus died for our sins and rose again that we would have life everlasting. It is by grace we are saved, it is by His unending love that we live, it is in Him that we are never alone in our lives. Just as the Garden is also ours, even as we also have a cross, even more so will we share in His glory as we follow Jesus in all things—we will see it and we will live it with Him. He has promised us this, "In my Father's house are many rooms" and "I am going there to prepare a place for you" (John 14:2). But before eternity is our cross. Before the cross is our Garden.

Picture the Garden in your mind—what do you see? Can you see its beauty? Can you see God's creative wonders? Can you picture the life that is around you? Can you also see the place of sorrow and anguish for our Savior? Can you picture a place of both death and new birth, each at the same time? Can you see the angel comforting Jesus as He awaits His cross? Most of all, can you see yourself in a place of deep desire and distress in your own life as you seek the will of the Father? If you can picture yourself broken in prayer in the Garden, seeking God in the anguish of your soul, then you must also know this—you are not alone in the Garden. Along with you is one who knows the same anguish, who also desperately sought the comfort of His Father, who also struggled against His own will in order to be obedient to His cross. If you can picture yourself in the Garden, see that Jesus Himself kneels beside you. Rather than an angel, it is your Savior who comforts you and guides you—through all of your life. Jesus said, "And surely I am with you always, to the very end of the age" (Matt. 28:20). This is always true for us, especially when we humbly and earnestly choose the Father's will as we take our own place in the Garden. Our life is as the Garden: that He would give us His joy, His comfort, and His love as we turn away from the world and turn only to our loving God.

II. THE WORD

CHAPTER 5

THE WORD

When God speaks to us in His love, He knows what our hearts need to hear. While prophecy is often thought of as foreknowledge of future events, our wonderful Father knows our circumstances and our needs, and He says many different and beautiful things to His children to bring us comfort, encouragement, guidance, and correction in our lives and for His kingdom. Prophecy is hearing God speak and then delivering the word of God so that others will know it. In other writings and teachings the gifts of the Holy Spirit, and of prophecy, have been expounded upon. This writing will not attempt to do likewise. However, what follows is a collection of Bible verses and prophetic words that require a level of explanation. Each of the prophetic words are complete messages the Lord spoke using a person's voice, and were recorded on a tape recorder as they were spoken. Later, the words were transcribed. In most cases the words were spoken in a church service or prayer meeting. A few of the words were not spoken when the Lord first brought them, but He brought them again at a later time when I was in prayer.

These words were also recorded, transcribed, and shared with others as the Lord allowed.

The work of the Holy Spirit brought the words. There were times when I was certain He would not speak but He has. There were other times when I desperately needed to hear His direction or assurance, times when I asked Him to speak but no word came. How I feel or what I think matters less than the fact that He loves us and wants to share His heart with His children. While "the spirits of prophets are subject to the control of prophets" (1 Cor. 14:32), it seems the prophet is more able to quench or disobey speaking the word than he or she is able to bring the word when they want to.

Speaking the word is an act of faith. The Bible tells us "prophecy never had its origin in the will of man, but men spoke from God as they were carried along by the Holy Spirit" (2 Pet. 1:21). While some may think the word is brought forth the night before a meeting, or is memorized and practiced in private before being shared in public, the words are almost always spontaneous. In most cases, the extent of what the Lord will say is not known by the one God will speak through until the word is released. The complete revelation is only made known as the word is spoken. It is up to the one being used by the Lord to be sensitive to His Spirit, to know that a word is to be spoken, and to begin to speak in faith and love for God so that the Holy Spirit will flow and His word will be released.

How the words come or how the person to be used is first impressed that a word is being spoken is not the same for each person or each occasion for that person. There are different levels of anointing that may bring a word.

In most cases, when the word is spoken to a large audience or is significant, perhaps a word of correction, there will be a greater sense of the Holy Spirit's presence and a greater unction to speak. Sometimes when the Lord speaks directly to an individual or a small group, the anointing is subtle and the word comes quietly.

For me, in most cases the word is preceded by a sense of His presence. I can feel my heart begin to beat stronger, my breath becomes shorter, and my hands may begin to shake. There have been times when His anointing was quite strong, or when His word would build within me as we waited for an opportunity to speak, such that His Spirit would flow in waves causing me to tremble and shake in my hands, legs, and body. As the Holy Spirit begins to bring the word, either the first few words to be spoken are impressed within the mind, or a vision is given. These are prompts to begin speaking which often increase in intensity until the word is released. As the person speaks, the Holy Spirit flows and brings the actual words line by line. For some words, a sentence of it would be spoken first and, when taking my next breath, the next line to be spoken would be inhaled from the Holy Spirit—I could actually feel His words flow into me as I breathed and as I spoke. Often, besides feeling the words of the Lord from the Holy Spirit flowing through me, I could also sense the deep emotions of the Lord's heart for what He was saying.

What follows are words the Lord has spoken to His children. These words are directly from the heart of our Lord. They reveal a Living God who sees us today in this moment—each of our circumstances, trials, and even our deepest emotions of the heart. The words reinforce that

Scripture is as alive today as it was the day God breathed it and man recorded it. The words, as with all true revelations from the Holy Spirit, are confirmed by the Holy Bible.

The Lord wants us to prepare the condition of our heart so that we might understand His Scripture and believe revelations of the Holy Spirit—and be able to know with certainty that Jesus is alive, that He does love us, that He knows and understands us, and that He still speaks into our lives today. The Bible is holy and timeless, and the Lord wants us to have a renewed love for His written Word as we place it within our hearts. Also, our Lord wants us to see that He is forever the same and still longs for us and wants us to have Jesus, the Living Word, within our hearts and our very being. His life for us is as the Garden: that we would look on things eternal, things that are everlasting, and that through it all we would live the will of the Father, we would receive the love of Jesus, and we would walk each step of our journey in life with the Holy Spirit. His life for us is as the Word: that the Lord is the Living Word who speaks to us in the moment, and whose love and character towards His children are forever great and unchanging.

CHAPTER 6

THE LORD, HE IS GOD

When all the people saw this, they fell prostrate
and cried, "The LORD—he is God! The LORD—
he is God!"

—1 KINGS 18:39

While there are times when we may feel comfortable with our Heavenly Father and how He sees us, if we could truly see the Lord and know Him for who He is, then more often we would not be as casual when we come unto His presence. Could our actions and decisions stand in the sight of our pure and loving God? And yet what we have done in our lives, our thoughts and unseen motives of the heart, are clearly seen and known by Him. The Lord is high above us in every way, and we know that our own righteousness and deeds do not do justice to who He is. Even as we love Him and want only to please Him, we fall short of His character and His goodness. Still, our Lord Jesus sacrificed everything that was His to give us the most precious gift—every unholy thought, each misguided step, all of our sins, are taken far away from us as we kneel before the cross of Jesus Christ.

Who is this God who would make such a way for us?

Who is the Lord whose love for us is complete and pure, and whose passion for us is beyond our ability to comprehend? He tells us who He is throughout His Holy Bible, and He continues to tell us this today. Although we do not see God with our eyes, He is always visible to us. Although we cannot hear the Lord with our ears, He continuously calls out our names and speaks into our lives.

In these passages from the Holy Bible and in these prophetic words, our Father reveals Himself as the awesome God that He is. From nothing, the Lord created everything. In Him there is no weakness, only perfect strength. He knows all things, even the events of our past and our future, all of our problems and concerns, our good points and where we need to change. Whatever He plans, He does. He is living. He is unchanging. And yet, our Lord shows the tenderness of His love, the sweetness of His character, and even sorrow and vulnerability for His little children He loves so dearly. Even though He is God, the Lord desires us. He calls us to His side. He is always near to us. He makes a way for us. He shapes and molds us so that our character and our nature become like His.

The desire of the Lord's heart is that we would know Him for who He is, and that in knowing Him we would draw near to Him and give Him our love—the love that He longs for and that He so deserves. God has chosen us for His children, and as we choose Him as our Lord and as our Father it brings great joy to His heart, so much joy that He even sings over us with all of heaven listening! What a wonderful Lord!

—◆◆◆—

I AM YOUR MOUNTAIN

—During a church service—

Exalt the LORD our God and worship at his holy
mountain, for the LORD our God is holy.
—PSALM 99:9

I am the Lord, and I am your God. And I would ask you this
question: who among you would undertake a long journey
to see the mountain, to look upon its greatness, to see its
height and its beauty, to see the peacefulness of the mountain meadow, to see the purity of the mountain stream, to
see the perfection of the mountain flower as you hold it in
your hand, and to see the majesty of the eagle as it soars
among the peaks of the mountain—who would undertake
a journey such as this, and stand before the mountain and
yet close his eyes that he would not see that which he has
longed for? Or, who would stand before the mountain with
his eyes closed and ask a companion to describe all that
is before him, that which he can freely see for himself if
he would only open his eyes? Even so, I am the mountain.
And I stand before you now. My right hand is upon your
heart and My left hand is upon your head, and I am here
that you would see Me. I do not call you as a church, or as
a congregation, for I know each of you by name. And I call
each of you as an individual—as My child. And I would ask
you to humble yourself before Me, to repent of your sins,
to know that I am God. Open your eyes that you would see.
Still your hearts and listen that you would hear My voice.
Soften your heart that I would fill it with My love. Come to

Me, My children. For I am already here. Come to Me. For I am waiting for you.

> Humble yourselves before the Lord, and he will lift you up.
>
> —JAMES 4:10

> Be still, and know that I am God; I will be exalted among the nations, I will be exalted in the earth.
>
> —PSALM 46:10

———

COME KNOW ME

—During a management meeting at a Fortune 500 company—

> In the beginning God created the heavens and the earth.
>
> —GENESIS 1:1

> He has made everything beautiful in its time. He has also set eternity in the hearts of men; yet they cannot fathom what God has done from beginning to end. I know that everything God does will endure forever; nothing can be added to it and nothing taken from it. God does it so that men will revere him.
>
> —ECCLESIASTES 3:11–14

> The wrath of God is being revealed from heaven against all the godlessness and wickedness of men who suppress the truth by their wickedness, since what may be known about God is plain to them, because God has made it plain to them. For since the creation of the world God's invisible qualities—his eternal

power and divine nature—have been clearly
seen, being understood from what has been
made, so that men are without excuse.

—ROMANS 1:18–20

I am the Lord, and I am your God. And you would ask Me
what I would say to you now? I tell you, it is right for you
to ask Me this question. For it is true, you do not know Me.
Can you know someone whom you have not seen? And can
you love someone whom you do not know? Even so, I am
the Lord and the entire universe lies at My feet. All of creation is the result of My word. Still, you do not know Me,
even though you should. For when you look upon the sky
at night and see the beauty of the moon as it shines its light
on the world and the multitude of stars scattered across the
sky, you would look in wonder at what you see. It is too big
and too wonderful for you to truly understand. And as you
look upon the sky during the day and see the beauty of the
blue of the sky against the white and grays of the clouds,
ever changing in shape and form as they gently move in the
wind across the sky, you would be speechless at the beauty
and the variety of what you see. It is too beautiful and
too magnificent for your words. And as you would stand
in the meadow of the mountain and see the form of the
rock and the splendor of the trees and flowers, the purity
of the mountain stream as it flows through the meadow,
and watch as the deer would walk silently through the long
grass, and as the breeze would gently caress your cheek and
hair, you would stand in awe of what you see. It is too glorious and too perfect in harmony for you to comprehend.
All of this is My creation. And it calls you to Me. For could
such beauty and such perfection have occurred by accident?

Did this magnificent world with its sky and mountains and trees and flowers and animals appear from nothing by its own will? Consider these things and examine your hearts, and you will know that I am God. Seek Me in your life, and I will reveal Myself to you. Listen, and you will hear My voice calling for you. Speak to Me and I will hear you. I will join you in an instant. I will show you the path of the righteous. For in all of My creation that I love, it is you I love the most. It is you I long to be with. It is you I call My children. It is you I call to Me now.

> But if from there you seek the LORD your God,
> you will find him if you look for him with all
> your heart and with all your soul.
>
> —DEUTERONOMY 4:29

> Whoever has my commands and obeys them,
> he is the one who loves me. He who loves me
> will be loved by my Father, and I too will love
> him and show myself to him.
>
> —JOHN 14:21

THE CARPENTER

—During a prayer meeting—

When the Sabbath came, he began to teach in the synagogue, and many who heard him were amazed. "Where did this man get these things?" they asked. "What's this wisdom that has been given him, that he even does miracles! Isn't this the carpenter? Isn't this Mary's son and the brother of James, Joseph, Judas and Simon? Aren't his sisters here with us?"

And they took offense at him.

—MARK 6:2–3

Yet, O LORD, you are our Father. We are the clay,
you are the potter; we are all the work of your
hand.

—ISAIAH 64:8

My children, many times in My life I would hold the
wood in My hand, and I would see the shape and its
form, yet I would put My hand to the task, and I would
take this wood, and I would shape it, and I would mold
it—for I was known as the carpenter. And so it was that
I would work with the wood; I would make it into something useful or something beautiful, but I would take the
raw form and I would change it. And carefully I would
chip away the parts that would not be used, the parts that
would not bring beauty, until what I had formed in My
mind was formed in the wood. And so it is in your lives,
My children, that even now I am still the carpenter and I
would take you in My hand, I would take your lives and
I would take your hearts, and I would see you in your
raw form —and yet I would see ahead. I would see you
as perfection. I would see you in the image that I would
shape with My own hand. And I would chip away, My
children. I would shape you and I would mold you. And
this is the life that you live, and it is the life that I live
with you. For truly every day I am with you, and I shape
you, and I mold you. The day will come and you will be
useful as there is need, and you will be beautiful as there
is need—for this is My desire. This is My desire for you.
This is My desire for your lives.

Your hands shaped me and made me.

—JOB 10:8

In a large house there are articles not only of gold and silver, but also of wood and clay; some are for noble purposes and some for ignoble. If a man cleanses himself from the latter, he will be an instrument for noble purposes, made holy, useful to the Master and prepared to do any good work.

—2 TIMOTHY 2:20–21

I can do everything through him who gives me strength.

—PHILIPPIANS 4:13

BEHOLD MY CREATION

—During a prayer meeting with many
people who were overwhelmed by problems—

The sea is his, for he made it, and his hands formed the dry land.

—PSALM 95:5

Should you not fear me? declares the LORD. Should you not tremble in my presence? I made the sand a boundary for the sea, an everlasting barrier it cannot cross. The waves may roll, but they cannot prevail; they may roar, but they cannot cross it.

—JEREMIAH 5:22

I am the Lord, and I am your God, and I would take you to the shoreline, to the place where the ocean meets the land, and you would stand in the sand and marvel at the beauty before you. You would see the power of the ocean as it would first gently rise and then suddenly lift into a mighty wave, rushing forward to touch the land. You would look beyond the waves to see the blue of the water, glistening with the reflecting light of the sun, as it would go on seemingly without end. You would see the glory of the sky, bright and blue from the sun, the whites and grays of the clouds constantly moving and changing in shape and form. You would see the variety of birds on the shore and flying around you, and you would hear their cries. You would hear the thunder of the waves as they would crash into the shore. And you would feel the coolness, the freshness of the wind as it would touch your face and hair. All of this is My creation, and you would know this to be true. You would stand in awe of what you see. You would think of its beauty and of its glory. You would see My great love and My strength and My power through all that is around you. Then, you would notice the sand of the beach, and you would reach down and hold the sand in your hand. You would think, "So great are the problems and the trials of this world." For they are greater in number than the grains of sand you would hold in your hand, as many as the grains of sand upon the shore. But I would speak to you. I would remind you that I am the Living God and that I am the same now as I was in the beginning of creation. For I know each of your problems, I know all of your trials—and I could name each of them even as I could name the number of grains of sand that you would hold in your hand. And I would say to you: be encouraged. Look all around you. Behold My creation. Behold this gift I have given you. And know that the beauty of My creation that surrounds you is greater than the weight of the sand that you would hold in your hand. Know that My love and the promise of the life you will have with Me for eternity exceed the weight of the problems and the trials of this world. And I would say to you, praise Me. Worship at My feet, for I am here. Praise Me, and you will see the beauty that surrounds you. Worship Me, and I will help you to see the glory that awaits you in heaven. Praise Me, and I will empty the sand from your hand. Worship Me, for I am the Lord.

> "I the LORD do not change. So you, O descendants of Jacob, are not destroyed.
>
> —MALACHI 3:6

> In this you greatly rejoice, though now for a little while you may have had to suffer grief in all kinds of trials. These have come so that your faith—of greater worth than gold, which perishes even though refined by fire—may be proved genuine and may result in praise, glory and honor when Jesus Christ is revealed. Though you have not seen him, you love him; and even though you do not see him now, you believe in him and are filled with an inexpressible and glorious joy, for you are receiving the goal of your faith, the salvation of your souls.
>
> —1 PETER 1:6–9

I AM WITH YOU

—At the conclusion of a church service—

I am with you and will watch over you wherever

you go, and I will bring you back to this land. I
will not leave you until I have done what I have
promised you.

—Genesis 28:15

I love those who love me, and those who seek
me find me.

—Proverbs 8:17

I am the Lord, and I am your God—and you are My children. It is you that I love, it is you that I love greater than
all of creation. And I would speak to you of love, for I
love you with all of My heart. I love you with the heart of
the Living God. Worry not if I would go with you. Think
not that I am within these walls only. Think not that I am
only within these songs that you have sung. For My eyes
are always upon you. My hand is always upon you. And
I am always with you. And as you leave this service this
evening, it is I who will walk beside you. It is I who will
go with you into this world. And I would say to you, be
encouraged. Be bold. Be strong. For the Living God walks
beside you.

I have given them your word and the world has
hated them, for they are not of the world any
more than I am of the world. My prayer is not
that you take them out of the world but that
you protect them from the evil one. They are
not of the world, even as I am not of it.

—John 17:14–16

I have given them the glory that you gave me,
that they may be one as we are one: I in them
and you in me.

—John 17:22–23

43

Therefore go and make disciples of all nations, baptizing them in the name of the Father and of the Son and of the Holy Spirit, and teaching them to obey everything I have commanded you. And surely I am with you always, to the very end of the age.

—MATTHEW 28:19–20

WE WILL BE AS ONE

—During a prayer meeting—

The sun has one kind of splendor, the moon another and the stars another; and star differs from star in splendor.

—1 CORINTHIANS 15:41

He determines the number of the stars and calls them each by name.

—PSALM 147:4

By the word of the LORD were the heavens made, their starry host by the breath of his mouth. He gathers the waters of the sea into jars; he puts the deep into storehouses. Let all the earth fear the LORD; let all the people of the world revere him. For he spoke, and it came to be; he commanded, and it stood firm. The LORD foils the plans of the nations; he thwarts the purposes of the peoples. But the plans of the LORD stand firm forever, the purposes of his heart through all generations.

—PSALM 33:6–11

My children, you would look upon the stars and their

light would shine bright upon you, and you would marvel at their beauty. You would marvel at the stars in the heavens, My children. You would see that there is no pattern to their place, there is no rhyme or reason to where they are—and yet they are, My children! And they are exactly where I placed them. I know their place. And at times, My children, your life would seem the same, that it would seem to randomly fall about you...no rhyme...no reason, and you would wonder what is the purpose and how is it that things have happened this way for you. And yet I tell you that I know your place. Even as I placed the stars in the heavens, yet I have placed you in this world. Even as the light shines from the heavens, yet the light shines in you, My children. For you I have chosen, you I have taken to My side, you I have filled with My love. And always it is My love for you that burns deep within Me; it is the aching of My heart—beyond what you know, beyond what you yourself have felt, so is My love for you. And know this, My children, that I am humble before you, that I am gentle with you, that in all things I desire good for you, and that as you give your-selves to Me, yet My hand stands before you, and I will protect you. The wind will not move a hair upon your head unless I would allow it, so closely will I stay to you, such will My protection be for you. Know this, My chil-dren, that as you look upon the stars and the glory fills your eyes, it does not compare to the glory that one day you shall see. For one day, My children, you will stand before Me, and you will look upon Me. It will not be as through the spirit, My children—it will be real, it will be in the moment and you will see Me; and the glory of the stars will pale in comparison for what you will see; and the feeling of love that you have for Me will pale in comparison for the love that will burn in your heart. For in that moment, the love that I have, the burning of My heart, it will be in your heart—we will be as one. And you will live this, My children. Each of you—you will live this. It will be a moment in your life even as this is a moment in your life, even as now you hear My words you will hear My words, and you will see My mouth move as I speak. This is My promise to you, My children. Stay close to Me. Stay close. Look upon the stars and know that it is a promise, My children—as real as the stars.

> Dear friends, now we are children of God, and what we will be has not yet been made known. But we know that when he appears, we shall be like him, for we shall see him as he is.
>
> —1 JOHN 3:2

> They will see his face, and his name will be on their foreheads. There will be no more night. They will not need the light of a lamp or the light of the sun, for the Lord God will give them light. And they will reign for ever and ever.
>
> —REVELATIONS 22:4–5

I AM THE WAY

—During a church service—

Jesus answered, "I am the way and the truth

and the life. No one comes to the Father except through me."
—John 14:6

Therefore Jesus said again, "I tell you the truth, I am the gate for the sheep. All who ever came before me were thieves and robbers, but the sheep did not listen to them. I am the gate; whoever enters through me will be saved. He will come in and go out, and find pasture. The thief comes only to steal and kill and destroy; I have come that they may have life, and have it to the full.
—John 10:7–10

But seek first his kingdom and his righteousness, and all these things will be given to you as well. Therefore do not worry about tomorrow, for tomorrow will worry about itself. Each day has enough trouble of its own.
—Matthew 6:33–34

My children, there is a way for you! There is a way, My children—for I am the way. I go before you, and I open the doors, and I walk that you would follow. There is a way, My children—I have made the way. I have come to this world and poured Myself out for you that there would be grace—there is forgiveness and there is mercy and love. So it is that I would say, Fear not for what would come, fear not for what lies ahead, fear not for what you would read or what you would imagine in your minds. For I tell you now, I am the way and I will make a way for you, My children—for your families. I am the way. Cling to Me. Cling fast to Me. I will walk before you, and as you would come with Me, as you would surrender yourself to Me, this is the way for you, My children: I will protect you, I will be with you, I will be your glory, I will be your joy, I will be your peace, My children. Know this now. Know this: that those whom I love I ask that you would work for Me and that you would live for Me, but I will be merciful and I will be kind to you, My children. I will be with you. I will guide you. Know this, My children. Know this and fear not. Let there be faith. Let there be faith, for there is much to have faith in, My children. You can have faith in Me and in My love for you.

> So do not fear, for I am with you; do not be dismayed, for I am your God. I will strengthen you and help you; I will uphold you with my righteous right hand. All who rage against you will surely be ashamed and disgraced; those who oppose you will be as nothing and perish. Though you search for your enemies, you will not find them. Those who wage war against you will be as nothing at all. For I am the LORD, your God, who takes hold of your right hand and says to you, Do not fear; I will help you.
>
> —ISAIAH 41:10–13

> But now, this is what the LORD says—he who created you, O Jacob, he who formed you, O Israel: "Fear not, for I have redeemed you; I have summoned you by name; you are mine. When you pass through the waters, I will be with you; and when you pass through the rivers, they will not sweep over you. When you walk through the fire, you will not be burned; the flames will not set you ablaze. For I am the LORD, your God, the Holy One of Israel, your Savior.
>
> —ISAIAH 43:1–3

The LORD will guide you always; he will satisfy your needs in a sun-scorched land and will strengthen your frame. You will be like a well-watered garden, like a spring whose waters never fail.

—ISAIAH 58:11

BELIEVE

—During a prayer meeting, following a discussion about how immoral the world is becoming—

He loads the clouds with moisture; he scatters his lightning through them. At his direction they swirl around over the face of the whole earth to do whatever he commands them. He brings the clouds to punish men, or to water his earth and show his love. "Listen to this, Job; stop and consider God's wonders. Do you know how God controls the clouds and makes his lightning flash? Do you know how the clouds hang poised, those wonders of him who is perfect in knowledge?

—JOB 37:11–16

My children, it is My peace I speak unto you! It is My peace I give to you. I would ask that you would not be confused. I would ask that you would not be offended by Me, and for who I am; you would not be offended by this world and how things are. For truly I say to you, My children, that as you look upon the clouds in the sky, you do not understand how they are formed, you do not know why they look the way they do, from where they come, to where they will go, you do not know why they dissipate and vanish into the air or what would happen as this occurs. You do not know, My children, and yet I tell you, you believe in the clouds—you know they are real. For what you have seen with your eyes, it is easy to believe, even though you would not know. And so it is with Me, My children. So it is for Me that as you would see Me you would know and you would believe—and yet you do not see…you do not know. And isn't this the test, My children? Is this not the test? Is this not the difficulty? Is this not why so many would not turn to Me? Why they would not believe? For if they had seen, if they had looked upon Me, if they could touch Me with their hands, they would know and they would believe—even as they believe that the clouds in the sky are real. And yet I do not work this way, My children. There is a choice—in all things a choice that you must make. It is My desire that you would become people of character, that you would be people of love and understanding and discernment. This is My desire, and yet it is a difficult path, My children. It is a difficult road. There are many turns that you would take, many forks in the road, and it is confusing—but this is My promise: that I am more real than the clouds, and the day will come and you will be before Me and all that is uncertain will be made clear. All that is unknown will be made known to you, My children. You will have no doubts, for you will know and you will know in your hearts and you will see Me. You will see Me! And this is My desire, My children: that you will see Me and that you will know, and that until that day you will cling to this promise. You will know that it is true now even before it happens for you. Have faith, My children. Be faithful. Do not become overly concerned in these matters. Do not allow it to stir up within you feelings of frustration or concern, for I tell you the truth—I am not frustrated. I am not concerned. My children, have faith, know that I am God—for truly, I am God.

> Then Jesus told him, "Because you have seen me, you have believed; blessed are those who have not seen and yet have believed."
> —JOHN 20:29

> Now we see but a poor reflection as in a mirror; then we shall see face to face. Now I know in part; then I shall know fully, even as I am fully known.
> —1 CORINTHIANS 13:12

WEAK BECOMES STRONG

—During a prayer meeting—

> But he said to me, "My grace is sufficient for you, for my power is made perfect in weakness." Therefore I will boast all the more gladly about my weaknesses, so that Christ's power may rest on me. That is why, for Christ's sake, I delight in weaknesses, in insults, in hardships, in persecutions, in difficulties. For when I am weak, then I am strong.
> —2 CORINTHIANS 12:9–10

> For we do not have a high priest who is unable to sympathize with our weaknesses, but we have one who has been tempted in every way,

just as we are—yet was without sin. Let us
then approach the throne of grace with confidence, so that we may receive mercy and find
grace to help us in our time of need.

—HEBREWS 4:15–16

Yet when I surveyed all that my hands had done
and what I had toiled to achieve, everything was
meaningless, a chasing after the wind; nothing
was gained under the sun.

—ECCLESIASTES 2:11

My children, you would speak of weakness, and each of
you would sense it within yourselves. You would think
of yourselves as weak for you would know that there is a
higher ground that you would stand upon and yet you do
not stand upon it. I tell you truth, My children—the word
weakness does not come to My mind. When I think of you, I
do not think of weakness, for I have walked this earth even
as you walk it, I have lived and breathed, even as you live
and breathe now, and I understand the trials of this world. I
understand what it is to live in a body; that your thoughts are
your own thoughts, your life is your own life. Even though
you would share with others—yet you are alone. I understand these things, My children. Weakness does not come to
My mind, for who would struggle with the wind and seek to
hold it, and not hold the wind and think themselves weak?
And surely this life is as chasing the wind if you would chase
it. But I say to you, do not chase the wind! Do not seek after
the wind of this world, but cling to Me, My children. For in
Me there is no weakness—there is strength, there is stead-
fastness, there is faithfulness. All these things are in Me, My
children. And as you cling to Me, so it is that My character is

given to you. I reveal Myself to you and you become as I am. And always, My children, it is with My love, it is with My affection—and My affection is for you. Do not worry about your lives and how you would live them, only seek after Me. Only know that I understand you, that I know you—and still I love you. And I will always love you. And this world is a fleeting moment in your lives, My children. It is but a fleeting moment—soon to be a memory of what you have done and what you have lived. A memory—as you stand in My presence, as you see Me and you feel Me, and what is unknown is revealed to you—and there is no weakness in this, My children! There is no weakness—and this is your future! Know this now, for each of you: I have claimed you. I have spoken your name, even as you have spoken mine. I have spoken your name, and even as you would pray this evening I sit at the right hand of the Father and I intercede for you. I speak to him of you. Fear not, My children. Worry not. You are mine. You are always mine.

> But seek his kingdom, and these things will be given to you as well.
> —LUKE 12:31

> Who of you by worrying can add a single hour to his life? Since you cannot do this very little thing, why do you worry about the rest?
> —LUKE 12:25–26

> Jesus Christ is the same yesterday and today and forever.
> —HEBREWS 13:8

> Cast all your anxiety on him because he cares for you.
> —1 PETER 5:7

———

DRAW CLOSE TO ME

*—During a church service, after the prayer leader prayed
about the glory of God in the stars—*

"To whom will you compare me? Or who is my
equal?" says the Holy One. Lift your eyes and
look to the heavens: Who created all these? He
who brings out the starry host one by one, and
calls them each by name. Because of his great
power and mighty strength, not one of them is
missing.

—ISAIAH 40:25–26

My children! My dear ones! You would hear of the stars,
the stars of the heavens; and consider My creation—consider the stars; for truly each one I spoke that it would be;
truly each one I placed in the heavens that it would have
its place; and truly there are stars that I know the eyes of
man have yet to see—and yet they are, for I have made
them. And I have made the stars that though the dark of
night would come, yet there would be light; that My children would never be without the light and the stars of the
heavens would be a sign and would be a guidance, that
people would find their way in the darkness; that even the
sailor on the vastness of the sea, yet he would know his
direction, he would know his path; and so it is that for a
dying world yet the stars are a sign that He who created
the stars yet lives—and He is greater than the stars for the
stars are My creation. And the stars are for you, My children, that though you would behold them, though you

would see their awesomeness, yet you would know that I am your God, yet you would know that I am closer to you than the stars. For truly, I have chosen you that you would know Me and that you would love Me. And even as I draw close to you, it is My desire that you would draw close to Me; that you would not see Me as the stars in the heaven, but you would know Me as the love of your heart; that My love would burn within you and that you would know Me and you would call Me by name, and for you, I am Abba. Abba, Father! Let My name come from your lips. Let My love be in your heart. Let My love be upon your life that I would protect you, that I would teach you, that I would draw you to Me. For truly, My children, I am in your hearts and even so, beyond the stars. Beyond the heavens—there I Am, My children. I Am. I Am.

> I keep asking that the God of our Lord Jesus Christ, the glorious Father, may give you the Spirit of wisdom and revelation, so that you may know him better. I pray also that the eyes of your heart may be enlightened in order that you may know the hope to which he has called you, the riches of his glorious inheritance in the saints, and his incomparably great power for us who believe. That power is like the working of his mighty strength, which he exerted in Christ when he raised him from the dead and seated him at his right hand in the heavenly realms, far above all rule and authority, power and dominion, and every title that can be given, not only in the present age but also in the one to come.
>
> —EPHESIANS 1:17–21

—◆—

HEAR MY SONG

—After singing a song at the conclusion of a prayer meeting—

How great is the love the Father has lavished on us, that we should be called children of God! And that is what we are!

—1 JOHN 3:1

The LORD your God is with you, he is mighty to save. He will take great delight in you, he will quiet you with his love, he will rejoice over you with singing.

—ZEPHANIAH 3:17

My children! I tell you the truth, My children, though you have not heard it, yet I would sing songs as well; yet I would lift My voice, and I would sing. From the depths of My heart, with the greatest of joy, song would burst forth from My mouth—for such is My love for you! Such is My love for you that as you would worship Me, as you would come to Me and empty yourselves for Me, yet I sing the song of thanksgiving and joy for how you would treat Me as your King and your Savior. They are songs of joy, My children, they come from My mouth, and it is as I watch you live your lives and you would give your lives to Me. It is of great importance to Me. It is of great joy to Me. And so I share this with you, My children, that you would bring a song into My heart, that you would cause Me to sing with great joy, for how you have loved Me this evening, how you have given to Me this evening. Is this not your reward, My children—that I would sing to you? For I tell you the truth, all of heaven hears My songs. Every angel would stop to listen to My voice as I would sing, and with great beauty My voice would ring out throughout the heavens; throughout the heavens yet My voice is heard, and I am singing your names, and I am singing love into your lives, and I am singing of you, and I am singing to you. It is My voice. It is My heart. It is My love.

> May our Lord Jesus Christ himself and God our Father, who loved us and by his grace gave us eternal encouragement and good hope, encourage your hearts and strengthen you in every good deed and word.
>
> —2 THESSALONIANS 2:16–17

SEPTEMBER 11, 2001—ATTACK ON AMERICA

—During a prayer meeting—

> The thief comes only to steal and kill and destroy; I have come that they may have life, and have it to the full.
>
> —JOHN 10:10

My children! I would speak to you now, for you are My children and such is My love for you—such is My love for you, My children! And I would see you as one who would stand in this world and all would seem safe, all would seem secure—all is as it should be. And you would stand before the lake and all is at peace: the water would be smooth as glass and it would reflect the beauty of the sky and the trees that would line its shore. You would marvel at its beauty, and you would possess it, as it is yours. And yet the stone has been cast, and the rock would fall, and with great violence it would crash into the water, and what was at peace is now disturbed. You would see the rock—and it would hit the water, and the water would rise up upon itself and fall back down. And nothing is as it was—as it seemed in your eyes, My children! And yet I tell you now, the rock has fallen and yet it has sunk in the water, and it will not be seen again. And what remains, My children, is upon the water, for there is a wake that would rise, and the ripples would spread in ever widening circles—even from where the rock would crash. And such is the work of Satan that he would cast the stone and yet he would not see what would happen after. He would not see the beauty as the water would widen in circles, and the wake would form, and the wake would broaden, and it would reach the near shore, and it would go to the far shore. It is My beauty, My children—again. It is the wave of My Spirit that even in the midst of this time, even in the midst of this disaster, in this attack—yet I prevail! Yet I complete My work, My children—for always it is My kingdom, and I work for My kingdom, My children, that My Spirit will spread out from this, and others will see it—people who would not see before, who would not look upon the lake before—yet now they will look and now they will see. It is My desire, My children, and already, already My work has been completed. For there were those whose bodies are now consumed by the fire, and yet I snatched them from the eternal fire, that before they were taken, yet they beheld their God, and they confessed their Lord, for such was My desire, My children, that none would be lost. And let this be your prayer, My children—let it be your faith:

that already I have overcome. Already My plans are victorious. It is My desire that this nation would rise up in one voice, and they would praise Me. This is My desire, My children—and yet Satan would have his own schemes. And so I say to you, continue in your prayers…praise My name…glorify Me…and pray the plans of Satan would fall to the ground, that they would be destroyed, or that his effects would be lessened; for so I say, he will try again and he would bring more against this nation, more against My people. And yet, even as he would not see the ripples on the lake, he does not see how I will take his plans and use them for My kingdom, use them to draw My children to Me. And yet let this be your faith: I will draw them, My children. They are Mine! I desire them, My children! I desire them even as I desire you. I love them even as I love you. Let this be your faith: that the peace of the lake is before you, and it will be restored. It is My kingdom, My children. It is My kingdom.

> In the same way your Father in heaven is not willing that any of these little ones should be lost.
> —MATTHEW 18:14

> In order that Satan might not outwit us. For we are not unaware of his schemes.
> —2 CORINTHIANS 2:11

> Finally, be strong in the LORD and in his mighty power. Put on the full armor of God so that you can take your stand against the devil's schemes.
> —EPHESIANS 6:10–11

September 12, 2001—The Day After

—During a church service—

The LORD has done what he planned; he has fulfilled his word, which he decreed long ago.

—Lamentations 2:17

Have you not heard? Long ago I ordained it. In days of old I planned it; now I have brought it to pass.

—Isaiah 37:26

I make known the end from the beginning, from ancient times, what is still to come. I say: my purpose will stand, and I will do all that I please.

—Isaiah 46:10

My children! What I have spoken, surely it will come to pass, and what has been planned, so it shall be, My children. And though I have seen the beginning and I have seen the end, even so, My children, in this moment, in this time, do I not share your grief? Is My heart not filled with sorrow even as you would be filled with sorrow? And I have compassion for you, My children; for you would live your life moment by moment not knowing or seeing what is to come, and as it would come it may bring great joy or it may bring great sorrow, and it is yours to live—it is yours to enjoy or yours to push through. And I have seen the beginning, and I have seen the end, and still I grieve with you, My children. Come to Me now, My children! Come to Me now! Let us comfort each other. Let Me be comforted by your love. Let Me be comforted that you would believe in Me, that you would not know what your future would hold, that you would not know what this world would bring against you, and though it would be filled with trial and difficulty and joy and hope, yet still your faith is in Me. This is My joy, My children. And let this be your joy: that regardless of what this world would have for you, regardless of its pleasures, regardless of its trials, yet as you would confess Me, as you would put your faith in Me, that your name is written in the Book of Life, and for all eternity you will be with Me. The time will come and you will stand with Me, and your future will be assured. You will still live moment by moment—and yet you will not worry! There will be no tears, My children. I will wipe these tears from your eyes. Even as you would cry now, yet you will be filled with joy. These are My words to you, My children: that always I have loved you and My love for you is unchanging; My love for you continues, and it is greater than you would think, it is more than you could know. Let this be your faith, My children: I have seen the end. Though you would live this day and it is but a day for you, and even in the next moment, you would not know the words that would come from My lips—yet already I have heard them, yet already I have seen, yet already I know the future, My children. For you…it is in My arms, My children. It is in My love. I am your future. Fear not for this world, and be comforted in this: that My love is for you. Receive My peace. Receive My comfort. Receive it, My children—for it is here for you and I am here for you.

> Those who sow in tears will reap with songs of joy. He who goes out weeping, carrying seed

to sow, will return with songs of joy, carrying
sheaves with him.

—PSALM 126:5–6

THESE ARE THE TIMES

—During a prayer meeting after discussion about
current events and the End Times—

He changes times and seasons; he sets up kings
and deposes them. He gives wisdom to the
wise and knowledge to the discerning.

—DANIEL 2:21

He replied, "When evening comes, you say, 'It
will be fair weather, for the sky is red,' and in
the morning, 'Today it will be stormy, for the
sky is red and overcast.' You know how to interpret the appearance of the sky, but you cannot
interpret the signs of the times."

—MATTHEW 16:2–3

From the days of John the Baptist until now,
the kingdom of heaven has been forcefully
advancing, and forceful men lay hold of it.

—MATTHEW 11:12

My children! You would speak tonight and you would
discuss the times in which you live. You would discuss My
Word and what it would say of these times. And it is wise
that you would have this conversation. It is good that you
would discuss these things. For truly these are the days in
which you live, and it does not help to not think about
it. It does not help to pretend that these times are not

here or that they will go away. It does not help to think that it is a future generation that will live this life and go through these times. For truly these are the times and you must be prepared. You must know the times in which you live—and you must live them, My children. Let this night be as a teaching to you, that as you discussed—it put a framework around your prayers, and it directed your prayers, for the kingdom moves forcefully forward for those who will take force and place their own hands upon it. This is My desire: that in your own hands you would hold the kingdom, that you yourselves would take force and you would help the kingdom to move forward—and it is as easy as this evening. For truly it is your prayers that I desire. It is your prayers from your heart that I see and that I respond to and that I work within. It is in your prayers and humility that I cloak you in the mantle that you would do the work that I have given you to do. And it is in requesting protection and the armor that I do indeed protect you, that though Satan would come against you, he would fail. These are the times, My children, that you would seek after Me. These are the times that you would know Me. These are the times that you would stay close to Me—closer than you have before, because these are troublesome times for those who do not know Me, for those who are not close to Me. These can be troublesome times, My children, and yet they are times of My choosing; they are times that have been spoken of, and they are times that will be, they are times that will come to pass—and you will stand before Me, and they will be in your past. You will see them as they happen, and you will know that it is a time that is gone, for now your time is with Me. And is this not your joy, My children? Is this not your hope? Know that it is real. Know that the home is prepared for you—it awaits you already, and I myself have walked through the rooms. I have anointed the doorways. I have made the bed. My children, the home is ready, and it awaits you. It is yours. It is for you. Let this be your faith as you live in these days. Let it be your joy as you see the world about you and the changes that it will go through. Do not be afraid. The home awaits you, My children. These very words were spoken of this evening, and I say them now that you would know that I heard. I say them now that you would know that it is true. And I say them now that you would be encouraged, that you would not grow faint, you would not be afraid, and that you would know, My children, that it is in your prayers that you will fight this battle. I will use you in other ways: you will see things happen in your life—but it begins in prayer, My children. It begins in the anointing of the Holy Spirit that you must carry within you and you must let flow through you for all the tasks that will be done, for all the things in this time that will come to pass. And then, as you stand with Me you will look on these times and you will know that it was not of your own doing, it was only My Holy Spirit that allowed you to do these things. It was My Holy Spirit for everything, My children.

> What I have said, that will I bring about; what I have planned, that will I do.
>
> —ISAIAH 46:11

> Do not let your hearts be troubled. Trust in God; trust also in me. In my Father's house are many rooms; if it were not so, I would have

told you. I am going there to prepare a place for you. And if I go and prepare a place for you, I will come back and take you to be with me that you also may be where I am.

—John 14:1–3

I am the vine; you are the branches. If a man remains in me and I in him, he will bear much fruit; apart from me you can do nothing.

—John 15:5

CHAPTER 7

RETURN TO ME

I have swept away your offenses like a cloud,
your sins like the morning mist. Return to me,
for I have redeemed you.

—ISAIAH 44:22

Since the very moment Adam departed from the will of God, the Lord's deep desire has been to restore His children to the shelter of His heart. He is not a man that He would turn away from us or forget us. He is a loving Father who longs for us and who works for our good. The Lord wants us to know Him and to walk with Him throughout our lives. We are completely His, and He is calling us back to Him. Still, even as Adam had a choice, so we too have a choice. We can choose the Lord and receive the salvation that Jesus humbly and courageously sacrificed Himself to give to us, or we can continue on in our lives without Him. Choosing Jesus brings the promises of God's redemptive work in our hearts for this life, and beyond this life an eternity in His presence. Living life apart from the Lord is like undertaking a long and treacherous journey without any knowledge of the destination or even an understanding of what along the way is real and what is true. Life apart from God is only shallow and meaningless activity and, since the Lord created us all to be eternal beings, eventually leads to absolute death—everlasting separation from Him.

At times, those of us who have already responded to the Lord can become confident in the knowledge that God is real, and that as we die and leave this life we will stand before Him and look into the eternity of His eyes and see the holiness of His being. We hear messages of repentance and a call to Christ and think it a good thing to say, but that we ourselves are beyond it since we have already received Jesus as Lord. Too often we are complacent in our walk with the Lord; we say we love Him, but we lack the passion and intimate relationship we had when our love was first new. For us too, the Lord is calling us back to Him. For us too, the Lord wants a change and a new birth in our hearts. There is still more of Him than we know, and too much of ourselves in our lives.

For the lost and for the saved alike, the Lord gently and continuously calls to us and speaks into our hearts. "Count the cost!" He says. "Count the cost of how you live your lives, that you are apart from me!" It is a call that we cannot ignore. In truth, it is a call that shakes us to the depths of our souls and our very being. The Lord has provided the way, the truth, and the life so that we know how to be saved—and it is fully revealed to us in His written and living Word. Through the Holy Bible the Lord has called us to repentance. He clearly tells us that He will cleanse us of all our sins. In Him there is no shame, no delay—only complete and immediate forgiveness and deliverance from sin. The way is shown to us in Scripture, and is laid hold of and lived out only through Jesus. In Jesus, we must find a deeper repentance in our own hearts. A repentance so deep that in love for our precious Savior we will hate sin and vigorously fight against it in our lives; a repentance so complete that we will no longer do anything that might hurt our dear Lord or take away the presence of the Holy Spirit from us. We must repent, because we honor Him, because we cannot live without Him, and, ultimately, because we love Him.

In the Holy Bible and in His spoken words today, the Lord is calling the lost and the saved alike to return to Him completely, to walk in obedience, to cleanse ourselves from all sin, and to forgive one another. The Lord reminds us that He is gentle, and kind, and humble towards all of His children, and yet there is a cost that we will all pay if we do not utterly abandon this life for Him. In Christ alone we are accepted and forgiven as we accept and forgive others. In Christ we can receive all of God's love and mercy. In returning to the Lord our hearts are made pure, our love made unconditional, our faith is made perfect and our minds are transformed, all because He places His own heart, His own mind, and His own Spirit within us. It is through the cross of Jesus that our lives have meaning and purpose, and that the destination of our journey is made known and its achievement assured.

As You Repent

—During a church service following a sermon on the kindness and sternness
of God, and a call to repentance—

It was just before the Passover Feast. Jesus knew
that the time had come for him to leave this world
and go to the Father. Having loved his own who

were in the world, he now showed them the full extent of his love. The evening meal was being served, and the devil had already prompted Judas Iscariot, son of Simon, to betray Jesus. Jesus knew that the Father had put all things under his power, and that he had come from God and was returning to God; so he got up from the meal, took off his outer clothing, and wrapped a towel around his waist. After that, he poured water into a basin and began to wash his disciples' feet, drying them with the towel that was wrapped around him. He came to Simon Peter, who said to him, "Lord, are you going to wash my feet?" Jesus replied, "You do not realize now what I am doing, but later you will understand." "No," said Peter, "you shall never wash my feet." Jesus answered, "Unless I wash you, you have no part with me." "Then, Lord," Simon Peter replied, "not just my feet but my hands and my head as well!" Jesus answered, "A person who has had a bath needs only to wash his feet; his whole body is clean. And you are clean, though not every one of you." For he knew who was going to betray him, and that was why he said not every one was clean.

—JOHN 13:1–11

Consider therefore the kindness and sternness of God: sternness to those who fell, but kindness to you, provided that you continue in his kindness.

—ROMANS 11:22

My children, I speak to you now of a moment in another man's life when he looked in My eyes and said, "No, never will you wash my feet. Never!" and he did not understand, and he stood in his pride. And such is the moment for you,

My children. For you have heard truth this day, that I am a God of love and of mercy; and even so, there is sternness, there is judgment. And such is the time in your life, such is the moment in your life, that I stand before you now in all of My love and all of My power. And even so, I would serve you, My children. I would kneel before you, and I would take your feet in My hand, and I would wash them—as you would repent, as you would humble yourselves. As you would allow Me, My children, I would take your feet—I will cleanse you. And I will be your Lord, and I will be your God—as you repent! Is your heart broken? Will I not mend it? Are you weary? Will I not give you rest? Will I not give you peace? Will I not give you the victory in this life? For I desire you, My children! I desire you! And as you turn to Me, it is then that I will use you. Your life will be for Me, and I will be for you, and the fruit will grow, My children. There will be fruit in your lives, fruit in this church, fruit for this world—for I am for this world, My children. But it begins in you. It begins with humility. It begins with repentance, My children—in your heart! In your heart!

> "Even now," declares the LORD, "return to me with all your heart, with fasting and weeping and mourning." Rend your heart and not your garments. Return to the LORD your God, for he is gracious and compassionate, slow to anger and abounding in love, and he relents from sending calamity.
>
> —JOEL 2:12–13

> Come to me, all you who are weary and burdened, and I will give you rest. Take my yoke upon you and learn from me, for I am gentle and humble in heart, and you will find rest for your souls. For

my yoke is easy and my burden is light.

—MATTHEW 11:28–30

I am the true vine, and my Father is the gardener. He cuts off every branch in me that bears no fruit, while every branch that does bear fruit he prunes so that it will be even more fruitful. You are already clean because of the word I have spoken to you. Remain in me, and I will remain in you. No branch can bear fruit by itself; it must remain in the vine. Neither can you bear fruit unless you remain in me. I am the vine; you are the branches. If a man remains in me and I in him, he will bear much fruit; apart from me you can do nothing. If anyone does not remain in me, he is like a branch that is thrown away and withers; such branches are picked up, thrown into the fire and burned. If you remain in me and my words remain in you, ask whatever you wish, and it will be given you. This is to my Father's glory, that you bear much fruit, showing yourselves to be my disciples.

—JOHN 15:1–8

LEAVE YOUR SINS WITH ME

—During a church service—

If there is a natural body, there is also a spiritual body.

—1 CORINTHIANS 15:44

But if serving the LORD seems undesirable to you, then choose for yourselves this day whom you will serve, whether the gods your forefa-

> thers served beyond the River, or the gods of
> the Amorites, in whose land you are living. But
> as for me and my household, we will serve the
> Lord.
>
> —Joshua 24:15

I am the Lord your God, and you are My creation. You are My dear ones, you are My children, and I created you of spirit and of flesh. I have given you the power of choice in your lives, that you would choose to glorify Me, that you would choose to honor and to love Me. Even so, each of you makes wrong choices; each of you has sin in your lives. But know now that there is no sin that you have committed that My eyes have not seen before. No matter how terrible you would consider your actions, there is nothing that will change My love for you. And I say to you now, come to Me and freely confess your sins; empty them at My feet. Do not feel ashamed nor feel that any fault is too small to bring to My attention. Be responsible for your choices and humble yourself before Me. As you do, you will find Me eager to accept you. You will find My arms ready to embrace you. You will find that I am a gentle and forgiving Father who loves His children, whose consuming desire is to bless all those who would repent and seek Me in their lives.

> If we claim to be without sin, we deceive our-
> selves and the truth is not in us. If we confess
> our sins, he is faithful and just and will forgive
> us our sins and purify us from all unrighteous-
> ness.
>
> —1 John 1:8–9

He who conceals his sins does not prosper,

but whoever confesses and renounces them finds mercy.

—PROVERBS 28:13

"Come now, let us reason together," says the LORD. "Though your sins are like scarlet, they shall be as white as snow; though they are red as crimson, they shall be like wool. If you are willing and obedient, you will eat the best from the land; but if you resist and rebel, you will be devoured by the sword." For the mouth of the LORD has spoken.

—ISAIAH 1:18–20

SEEK THE MOUNTAIN

—During a prayer meeting—

Send forth your light and your truth, let them guide me; let them bring me to your holy mountain, to the place where you dwell.

—PSALM 43:3

The mountains will bring prosperity to the people, the hills the fruit of righteousness.

—PSALM 72:3

My children, many are My sons and many are My daughters whom I would take to see the glory of the meadow of the mountain. They would stand in the meadow, and they would look upon the glory of the mountain. They would look in awe at its greatness, at its strength, at its beauty. And they would see the stream of the mountain as it would fall down from the mountain. They would know that the stream would bring them life. And they would know that this is where they would want to be, where they would want to live their lives. So they would seek to build their homes in the meadow. They would build their homes before the mountain, and they would put up the walls. They would put coverings over the windows, and they would close the door. They would build their fire in the fireplace, and they would sit before it and feel that they were warm—that they were safe. And they would become comfortable. They would live within their home and they would forget to look upon the mountain, to seek the mountain. And they would live within their home, by themselves, they would live with all their own thoughts. They would hold on to their pride, and their anger, and their unforgiveness. They would forget to drink of the stream of the mountain for its life. My children, I am the mountain, and your hearts are the home that you would build. I am asking you now to seek the mountain, to go to your windows and open them, that the wind from the mountain would enter your heart. Open the door so I can enter your heart, that you would be released from your own heart, from your sin, and stand once again in the glory of the meadow, that you would look upon the mountain and seek Me. Seek Me, My children. Release all that you would hold within your heart to Me. For I am ready to receive it. I am ready to receive your heart. I am ready to forgive you, to renew you, to anoint you, to bless you. And so it shall be, that as you would open your heart to Me, as you would seek Me with all of your heart, that I will fill you and I will change you—you will become more than you are now, you will grow and become bigger. You will grow so that even as you would try, as you would stand before the door of the home that you had built, you will not be able to walk back through that door. You will have become too big to walk back to where you lived before. You will not go back to the home that you had built for your own comfort. You will stay in the meadow; you will stay in My presence. And you will be with Me and live with Me even as I am with you and live within you. Seek Me, My children. Open your hearts, and seek Me.

> For where your treasure is, there your heart will be also.
>
> —LUKE 12:34

> On this mountain he will destroy the shroud that enfolds all peoples, the sheet that covers all nations; he will swallow up death forever. The Sovereign LORD will wipe away the tears from all faces; he will remove the disgrace of his people from all the earth. The LORD has spoken.
>
> —ISAIAH 25:7–8

COUNT THE COST

—During the 1998 Fabless Semiconductor Association (FSA) Anniversary dinner, while Senator Bill Bradley was delivering the keynote address—

> "The God who made the world and everything in it is the Lord of heaven and earth and does not live in temples built by hands. And he is not served by human hands, as if he needed anything, because he himself gives all men life and breath and everything else. From one man he made every nation of men, that they should inhabit the whole earth; and he determined the times set for them and the exact places where

they should live. God did this so that men would seek him and perhaps reach out for him and find him, though he is not far from each one of us. 'For in him we live and move and have our being.' As some of your own poets have said, 'We are his offspring.' "Therefore since we are God's offspring, we should not think that the divine being is like gold or silver or stone–an image made by man's design and skill. In the past God overlooked such ignorance, but now he commands all people everywhere to repent. For he has set a day when he will judge the world with justice by the man he has appointed. He has given proof of this to all men by raising him from the dead."

—Acts 17:24–31

Blessed is the man whose sin the Lord does not count against him and in whose spirit is no deceit.

—Psalm 32:2

I am the Lord, and I am your God, and you are My children, you are My dear ones. I would watch you as you live your lives, I would watch you as you walk in this world, and I call each of you. I call each of you by name. Even so, most of you do not even know Me. Many of you who do, do not live your lives with Me, even though I seek to live My life with you. So it is, that I would know your name, but you would not know Mine. Yet I am the Living God. You are a people who look upon the stars at night and you would see their beauty, you would see their glory, and you would see that they would go on and on as if without end, and they would be too numerous to count. Yet, in your minds, you would try to count them, you would seek to understand, to explore, to number the stars. Yet I stand before you now, and I ask you to count the cost of your lives and how you live them. Consider your lives, for truly I say, they are as but a moment. The times in this world are as a second compared to eternity, compared to the true extent of your lives. And yet, you would not seek Me in this life, yet you would not live this life for Me. So it is that for eternity, you would be separated from Me, you would not know My love—you would be banished from My presence. And I say again, count the cost, My children, of how you are living your lives and turn to Me! For I stand before you now, and I call you by name that you would know Me, that you would love Me—for I love you! So it is, My children, that you have heard My words, you have heard Me speak. These words will liberate some, they will mean salvation for some of you, and yet for others, these words are as a sword. For on that day when you stand before Me, yet these words will come to your mind and it will be judgment for you if you have not turned to Me, if you have not sought Me in your lives, if you would not put your trust and faith in Me. So it is, My children, that I have now spoken to you words from My own mouth, words that are faithful, words that are true, words for you to consider, words for you to live your life by. So it is, My children, that the mouth of the Lord has spoken.

> Then he called the crowd to him along with his disciples and said: "If anyone would come after me, he must deny himself and take up his cross and follow me. For whoever wants to save his life will lose it, but whoever loses his life for me and for the gospel will save it. What good is it for a man to gain the whole world, yet forfeit his

soul? Or what can a man give in exchange for his soul? If anyone is ashamed of me and my words in this adulterous and sinful generation, the Son of Man will be ashamed of him when he comes in his Father's glory with the holy angels."

—MARK 8:34–38

Just as man is destined to die once, and after that to face judgment, so Christ was sacrificed once to take away the sins of many people; and he will appear a second time, not to bear sin, but to bring salvation to those who are waiting for him.

—HEBREWS 9:27–28

MY OPEN ARMS AWAIT YOU

—During a sermon on giving everything to follow Christ, while the Steven Curtis Chapman song, "For the Sake of the Call" was played—

One of those days Jesus went out to a mountainside to pray, and spent the night praying to God. When morning came, he called his disciples to him and chose twelve of them, whom he also designated apostles: Simon (whom he named Peter), his brother Andrew, James, John, Philip, Bartholomew, Matthew, Thomas, James son of Alphaeus, Simon who was called the Zealot, Judas son of James, and Judas Iscariot, who became a traitor.

—LUKE 6:12–16

That which was from the beginning, which we have heard, which we have seen with our eyes, which we have looked at and our hands have touched–this we proclaim concerning the

Word of life. The life appeared; we have seen
it and testify to it, and we proclaim to you the
eternal life, which was with the Father and has
appeared to us. We proclaim to you what we
have seen and heard, so that you also may have
fellowship with us. And our fellowship is with
the Father and with his Son, Jesus Christ.

—1 JOHN 1:1–3

My children. My dearest children. I would ask you to
remember a time long ago when My own feet walked upon
the soil of this world, and My feet were the same as your
own; when with My own lungs I breathed the air of this
world and the air would fill Me and give Me life, and My
lungs were the same as your own; when with My own eyes I
looked upon the beauty of this world, the beauty of creation,
and My eyes were the same as your own. And My eyes were
filled with tears of joy as I looked upon My children. And as
I watched them, I knew those that were Mine. I knew those
who would come to Me. And I spoke to them. I called them
by name. And they came to Me. They walked into My open
arms. They felt the grip of My hand in greeting. They felt
the embrace of My arms and the strength of My shoulders
as we would hold each other and My love would flow into
them. And through this time with My children, their lives
were changed completely. Though they would know struggles, though they would know trials and persecution, they
were as new people, and they would never go back to what
they had been before. They willingly put aside everything
that was theirs from this world so that they would have a
place with Me, for they had seen the Living God. They had
touched and heard the words of the Living God and it filled
them with power and conviction. No one could take away

that which they knew to be true. And I am true. And I tell you now, that even as it was for My first disciples, it is the same for you now. For I stand before you and I watch you in this world. And My eyes are filled with tears of joy, for I know that you are Mine. I know that you will come to Me when I call. And I call you to Me now. I am ready to greet you with My own hand. I am ready to receive you into My open arms. And I am ready to pour My love into you. I am ready to reveal Myself to you, that you would see Me and know Me even as My disciples did when I walked with them. And this is what I ask of you now, that you take your heart and place it aside so that I can replace it with My own; that you take your mind and place it aside so that I can replace it with My own; that you take your words and place them aside so that I can replace them with My own—and I will fill you with My own love and My own strength and My own power. And you will be as new people; you will be completely changed. You will pray and you will witness with the anointing of My Spirit. And you will be amazed at what will be done in My name. Are you ready, My children? For I speak your name. Are you ready, My children? For I call to you. Are you ready, My children? For I am ready to receive you into My open arms. Come to Me, My children. Come to Me, My dear ones. Come to Me.

> But whatever was to my profit I now consider loss for the sake of Christ. What is more, I consider everything a loss compared to the surpassing greatness of knowing Christ Jesus my Lord, for whose sake I have lost all things. I consider them rubbish, that I may gain Christ and be found in him, not having a righteous-

ness of my own that comes from the law, but that which is through faith in Christ–the righteousness that comes from God and is by faith. I want to know Christ and the power of his resurrection and the fellowship of sharing in his sufferings, becoming like him in his death, and so, somehow, to attain to the resurrection from the dead.

—PHILIPPIANS 3:7–11

Then Peter, filled with the Holy Spirit, said to them: "Rulers and elders of the people! If we are being called to account today for an act of kindness shown to a cripple and are asked how he was healed, then know this, you and all the people of Israel: It is by the name of Jesus Christ of Nazareth, whom you crucified but whom God raised from the dead, that this man stands before you healed. He is "'the stone you builders rejected, which has become the capstone.' Salvation is found in no one else, for there is no other name under heaven given to men by which we must be saved." When they saw the courage of Peter and John and realized that they were unschooled, ordinary men, they were astonished and they took note that these men had been with Jesus.

—ACTS 4:8–13

WHERE YOU MUST GO

—During a prayer meeting—

Then they spit in his face and struck him with their fists. Others slapped him and said,

"Prophesy to us, Christ. Who hit you?"

—MATTHEW 26:67–68

Jesus said, "Father, forgive them, for they do not know what they are doing." And they divided up his clothes by casting lots.

—LUKE 23:34

But I tell you, Do not resist an evil person. If someone strikes you on the right cheek, turn to him the other also.

—MATTHEW 5:39

Be kind and compassionate to one another, forgiving each other, just as in Christ God forgave you.

—EPHESIANS 4:32

My daughter, I looked into the eyes of a man and as I looked upon him, yet he spat in My face. As I looked upon him, yet his hand rose and fell across My face. And yet again I looked upon him and I saw My son, and I knew that I would die for him, that his sins would be upon Me—and yet I loved him. And yet My love for him knew no bounds, and there was nothing I would not do, for soon I would die for him—and he did not know and he did not understand. My daughter, I speak to you, and I speak to all who will hear and all who will seek Me, that this is the place to which you must journey. This is the place to which I have called you, that though one would stand before you and spit in your face, yet you must still love him; though one would raise his hand and strike your face, still you must love him. I know how hard this is. Do I ask for something that is simple? No! Yet I ask for your heart, yet I ask for your life, that you might live and that you might know Me! And so I ask, forgive one another. Forgive and repent of your own sins. For who would you look upon and know that you are better than he? In whom would you see sin and know that you yourself have not sinned? And so as you would stand before Me, as you would stand before a holy God, yet you must repent and you must seek love in your heart, for this is how I will take you beyond this place. This is how you will journey beyond this place, My daughter. And this is where you must go.

> Be completely humble and gentle; be patient, bearing with one another in love. Make every effort to keep the unity of the Spirit through the bond of peace.
>
> —EPHESIANS 4:2–3

> Bear with each other and forgive whatever grievances you may have against one another. Forgive as the Lord forgave you. And over all these virtues put on love, which binds them all together in perfect unity.
>
> —COLOSSIANS 3:13–14

> You, therefore, have no excuse, you who pass judgment on someone else, for at whatever point you judge the other, you are condemning yourself, because you who pass judgment do the same things. Now we know that God's judgment against those who do such things is based on truth. So when you, a mere man, pass judgment on them and yet do the same things, do you think you will escape God's judgment?
>
> —ROMANS 2:1–3

—※—

You Are Unique

—During a church service—

Generations come and generations go, but the earth remains forever. The sun rises and the sun sets, and hurries back to where it rises. The wind blows to the south and turns to the north; round and round it goes, ever returning on its course. All streams flow into the sea, yet the sea is never full. To the place the streams come from, there they return again. All things are wearisome, more than one can say. The eye never has enough of seeing, nor the ear its fill of hearing. What has been will be again, what has been done will be done again; there is nothing new under the sun.

—Ecclesiastes 1:4–9

My children, consider now My creation, for all things are similar and yet everything is unique in itself; for you would see the sun rise and the sun set; each day the sun is faithful and true—and it would be the same. And yet I speak truth, not one sunrise is as the next; each one is unique unto itself. And such is My creation—and such are you, My children. For each one of you, I have designed your bodies, I have designed your minds, and each of you is the same—and yet each is different. For I tell you the truth, since Adam, no one is as you. And I have made you according to My heart. I have made you unique. And I love you as you are. I love you as you will be as you seek Me and you love Me. There is no sin in your life that I have not seen before. There is nothing you have done that I cannot forgive—for those who would humble

85

THE GARDEN AND THE WORD

themselves and seek Me. There is nothing you would do that if you would take up My cross and follow Me that you would fail. For I am the Lord your God, and I do not fail. And you are My loved ones. You are My life. I place Myself in you. Let this be your faith, My children, let this be your faith: that the work of the cross was complete, that your sins are forgiven as you would receive Me and you would seek Me—and in Me there is no failure. In Me there is no loss for this world for I am all things for you, My children. I am all things for you.

> Where can I go from your Spirit? Where can I flee from your presence? If I go up to the heavens, you are there; if I make my bed in the depths, you are there. If I rise on the wings of the dawn, if I settle on the far side of the sea, even there your hand will guide me, your right hand will hold me fast. If I say, "Surely the darkness will hide me and the light become night around me," even the darkness will not be dark to you; the night will shine like the day, for darkness is as light to you. For you created my inmost being; you knit me together in my mother's womb. I praise you because I am fearfully and wonderfully made; your works are wonderful, I know that full well. My frame was not hidden from you when I was made in the secret place. When I was woven together in the depths of the earth, your eyes saw my unformed body. All the days ordained for me were written in your book before one of them came to be. How precious to me are your thoughts, O God! How vast is the sum of them! Were I to count them, they would outnumber the grains of sand. When I awake, I am still with you.
>
> —PSALM 139:7–18

Now faith is being sure of what we hope for

and certain of what we do not see.

—HEBREWS 11:1

All a man's ways seem innocent to him, but motives are weighed by the LORD. Commit to the LORD whatever you do, and your plans will succeed.

—PROVERBS 16:2–3

LET THE WALLS COME DOWN

—During a prayer meeting—

The heart is deceitful above all things and beyond cure. Who can understand it? "I the LORD search the heart and examine the mind, to reward a man according to his conduct, according to what his deeds deserve."

—JEREMIAH 17:9–10

So justice is far from us, and righteousness does not reach us. We look for light, but all is darkness; for brightness, but we walk in deep shadows. Like the blind we grope along the wall, feeling our way like men without eyes. At midday we stumble as if it were twilight; among the strong, we are like the dead.

—ISAIAH 59:9–10

My children, there are many in this life and there are many in this world who would not come to Me, and they would not know me—and it is of their own choice! They have chosen, for they would see the cost; they would see what they must give and what they must leave behind, and so it is that they would build the walls that would keep Me from them and block Me from their lives. And they do not see that the very walls that they would build are their own death. It is the prison that would bind them and it would kill them. And these are My words to you, My children, that blessed are you that you have heard My call and that you have come to Me. But even so, are there not walls in your own hearts? Are there not walls in your own lives? And I call you now to a deeper repentance, a repentance of the heart, My children; that you would see yourselves and you would see yourselves in death, My children; that you would die to yourself and give to Me and you would purge the evil that is within you. It is easy to do this, My children—yet it would be impossible, for you cannot do it on your own. And yet you must speak My name—that is all you must do, My children. Bow your heart to Me and call on My name: call on My name for forgiveness, and so it is that you are forgiven—and so it is that I can use you. And this is My desire in your lives, My children, that you would walk with Me and you would know My Spirit and you would know My power, My children, for you have not felt My power to the degree that I would give it to you. Let the walls come down in your lives, My children. Let them come down for Me. Let them come down, and I will bless you, and I will restore you, and I will renew you, and I will build you, My children, beyond your dreams, beyond your knowledge, for beyond all things, My children—I Am! I Am, My children! I Am!

> Therefore this is what the LORD says: "If you repent, I will restore you that you may serve me."
>
> —JEREMIAH 15:19

> "…and call upon me in the day of trouble; I

will deliver you, and you will honor me."

—Psalm 50:15

Moses said to God, "Suppose I go to the Israelites and say to them, 'The God of your fathers has sent me to you,' and they ask me, 'What is his name?' Then what shall I tell them?" God said to Moses, "I AM WHO I AM. This is what you are to say to the Israelites: 'I AM has sent me to you.'"

—Exodus 3:13–14

Forgiveness

—During a church service—

This, then, is how you should pray: "Our Father in heaven, hallowed be your name, your kingdom come, your will be done on earth as it is in heaven. Give us today our daily bread. Forgive us our debts, as we also have forgiven our debtors. And lead us not into temptation, but deliver us from the evil one." For if you forgive men when they sin against you, your heavenly Father will also forgive you. But if you do not forgive men their sins, your Father will not forgive your sins.

—Matthew 6:9–15

The fear of the LORD is the beginning of knowledge, but fools despise wisdom and discipline.

—Proverbs 1:7

My children, I speak to you now of a day in My own life, of a moment when I was high and lifted up; when My hands were stretched forth—for you, My children, for My love that took Me to this place, for My love that held Me to the cross. For I tell you now, My children, that My work was complete on the cross. My work was complete—that your sins would be forgiven, that there would be salvation and restoration for you. Can it be, My children? Can it be that you would come to the cross and you would ask forgiveness yet in your hearts you would not forgive others? Yet in your own heart you would carry the offense and the offense would consume you and consume your life? And I say again, My work on the cross was complete, and it was for you, My children. Receive My blood. Receive My sacrifice. Do not disdain My work on the cross. Do not disdain My sacrifice and what I gave. For I gave it all for you, My children: for the love of My Father, for My love for My sheep—and I count you as My sheep, My dear ones. I count you. Please, please forgive as I have forgiven. Forgive, My children. Empty your hearts. Empty your hearts of the offense that you would carry and give it to Me. Give to Me, My children, and carry it no longer. Carry it no longer, My children.

> And when you stand praying , if you hold anything against anyone, forgive him, so that your Father in heaven may forgive you your sins.
>
> —MARK 11:25

> Do not judge, and you will not be judged. Do not condemn, and you will not be condemned. Forgive, and you will be forgiven.
>
> —LUKE 6:37

Standard of Holiness

—During Communion Sunday church service—

I make known the end from the beginning, from ancient times, what is still to come. I say: my purpose will stand, and I will do all that I please.
—ISAIAH 46:10

Then he took the cup, gave thanks and offered it to them, saying, "Drink from it, all of you. This is my blood of the covenant, which is poured out for many for the forgiveness of sins.
—MATTHEW 26:27–28

I will sprinkle clean water on you, and you will be clean; I will cleanse you from all your impurities and from all your idols. I will give you a new heart and put a new spirit in you; I will remove from you your heart of stone and give you a heart of flesh. And I will put my Spirit in you and move you to follow my decrees and be careful to keep my laws.
—EZEKIEL 36:25–28

My children, I speak truth to you now, that even in this moment that I am greater than you would know; I am greater than you would think. For before you took your first breath, yet I had a plan for your life. Before you first saw light, yet I saw each day of your life stretch forth before you. Before your time, My children, yet I was. And I speak to you now that you would know the standard before you is a standard that I would set—that you would be holy, for I am the Lord who makes you holy. And it is through the cross it is through

91

My own sacrifice, that this is possible; that you would take your life and you would give it to me; that you would take the thoughts in your mind, which I hear even as though you would speak them to Me, and you would allow My blood to cleanse them; that you would take the lusts and cares of this world and place them aside. For the standard, My children, is a standard I have set for you—it is that you would be holy. Be holy for I am holy. Be holy, for the cross would make you holy. Let that be your thought tonight as you would partake in communion: that My blood cleanses you, and that there is no sin that you have committed that I have not seen, that I do not know—and yet I love you! My love for you remains unchanged! My love for you is unending, My children! Receive My love this evening. Receive forgiveness. Be holy and I will use you, My children. Desire Me and you will serve Me. Come to Me and I will come to you.

> Be perfect, therefore, as your heavenly Father is perfect.
>
> —MATTHEW 5:48

> But just as he who called you is holy, so be holy in all you do; for it is written: "Be holy, because I am holy."
>
> —1 PETER 1:15–16

> This is the message we have heard from him and declare to you: God is light; in him there is no darkness at all. If we claim to have fellowship with him yet walk in the darkness, we lie and do not live by the truth. But if we walk in the light, as he is in the light, we have fellowship with one another, and the blood of Jesus, his Son, purifies us from all sin.
>
> —1 JOHN 1:5–7

CHAPTER 8

AWAKE! AWAKE!

Awake, awake! Clothe yourself with strength,
O arm of the Lord; awake, as in the days gone
by, as in generations of old.

—ISAIAH 51:9

As the Holy Bible records the history of man and the Lord's workings to save His children, we see throughout that man has usually lived apart from our loving God. Even following times when the Lord has done great and mighty things revealing Himself clearly to His people as the Lord, far too soon we have lost our faith and love for Him, or have moved away from our only Father. Even as the Lord brought the glorious Messiah to His people Israel, even as they looked into His eyes and heard His words, most were unable to see and were unable to hear our Lord in Jesus. The Lord remains faithful and true through time, and His voice resounds throughout this world calling us back to Him. At times He moves with great force and power to show us that He is God, and too often we are unable to hear or understand Him. Even now, God the Father remains a mystery to His beloved children.

Now is the time for God's church to rise up in greater

love, in greater faith, and with a greater hope in Christ. Now is the time that God wants His people to move in faith and in understanding—an understanding of who God is and what His purposes are for this time, and an understanding for who we are in Christ Jesus. Throughout the Holy Bible we are told to seek after the Lord. The Lord's words remain the same in this day. The Lord is calling us to seek after Him more than we ever have before. He wants us to abandon everything in this life so that we can live a life of complete freedom. Freedom from sin, freedom from worry, freedom from hurt and pain, freedom from sickness—freedom found only in Him.

Now is God's time for His church to come together in greater love for Him, and to show our love as we attack every dividing wall in our lives that separates us from Him. The Lord is calling us to a renewed and passionate prayer life. He wants us to have a great desire for the Bible and to place His Word within our minds and hearts—to cherish and to believe His Word as the mighty stronghold and great weapon it is. He wants us to know Him, to learn His ways, and to grow in Him. The God of heaven and earth is asking His creation to believe in Him so that He can use us in greater ways for His kingdom. The Lord wants us to walk in the power and anointing of the Holy Spirit so that we will be victorious in every circumstance in our lives. Our Lord who gives life to everything that has life is asking us to die completely to ourselves and to live for Him alone. The Good Shepherd wants us to find His lost sheep for Him.

The Lord assures us in His words from the Holy Bible and from His prophecies today that by awakening in Him and by being obedient to His call there are great blessings: He will anoint us anew in His Spirit, and we have new life in Him; He has a plan for each of our lives, and we will live it out for Him; He is victorious over every scheme and move of Satan; He will be with us in every circumstance and situation; we will hear His voice, and He will show us the way in our lives; He will prosper us in Him. Beyond any motivation that may be our own, the Lord wants to release His Spirit upon us and wants us to walk in victory for the purposes of His kingdom. The time for this age is drawing to a close. Jesus is coming back for His people, and He is asking us to live each day as though His coming is today. He does not want us to conform to this world for another moment, but He wants to use us to transform the world in Him. For this to happen there must be a change in the church, and for this change to come there must be an awakening greater than has yet been seen in our time, because the saving of the lost that the Lord is about to bring will be the greatest work of His church in history. The Lord says He is coming soon. Awake, awake! For He is coming. Even so, come Lord Jesus! Come!

THIS IS THE TIME

—During a church service—

I will lie down and sleep in peace, for you alone,
O LORD, make me dwell in safety.

—PSALM 4:8

In a dream, in a vision of the night, when deep

sleep falls on men as they slumber in their beds,
he may speak in their ears and terrify them with
warnings, to turn man from wrongdoing and
keep him from pride, to preserve his soul from
the pit, his life from perishing by the sword.

—JOB 33:15–18

Awake, awake! Rise up, O Jerusalem,

—ISAIAH 51:17

My children! My dear ones! So close am I to you—closer than you can know; for every night I would hold you in My hands, and I would hold you to My breast that My love would be upon you, that My peace would be upon you, and that you would sleep, My children. Even as you would sleep you would be in My arms, and I would send you to rest in your bed and tuck you in. Yet even in your sleep, My children, your mind would race and the dreams would come, and you would awaken in the terror of the night. "Ah!" you would say, "It is but a dream! It is but a dream! Go back to sleep—it is but a dream." And yet I tell you now, My children, that never in time has a people known time as you do now. You carry the time on your wrists. You have put the calendar on your wall. You know the season. You know the time. Know the time in which you live, My children! Understand the time—that it is not as a dream! This is the time, My children, that I am calling My church! This is the time that I would awaken My children! It is not a dream, My children. Awaken, O church! Awaken, My children! This is the time that you would seek after me! This is the time that you would pray, that you would know Me, that I would place My Spirit upon you—I am in you and you are in me! This is the time, My children, that the light would be within you and the light would shine from you and though the darkness would rise against My people, yet the light would cause the darkness to flee! This is the time, My children! And for you to be ready you must pray, you must spend time with Me, you must read the Bible that My Word would be within you and truth would reign in your life! This is the time, My children! And as you spend time with Me, I speak truth to you – there is no fear for these times. There is no fear. These are the times of My choosing! It is the time of My will! They are times that have been written of, they are times that have been spoken. There is no fear for My children. Rise up My church! Awaken My children! For it is time. It is time.

> And do this, understanding the present time. The hour has come for you to wake up from your slumber, because our salvation is nearer now than when we first believed.
>
> —ROMANS 13:11

> The LORD Almighty has sworn, "Surely, as I have planned, so it will be, and as I have purposed, so it will stand.
>
> —ISAIAH 14:24

> Arise, shine, for your light has come, and the glory of the LORD rises upon you. See, darkness covers the earth and thick darkness is over the peoples, but the LORD rises upon you and his glory appears over you.
>
> —ISAIAH 60:1–2

———◆———

FEAR NOT

—Before a prayer meeting we had looked at a giant spider web. Someone
created a wave of wind with her hand, and the web
had partially disintegrated. She then blew on it and it was gone.—

No weapon forged against you will prevail.

—ISAIAH 54:17

"For I know the plans I have for you," declares
the LORD, "plans to prosper you and not to
harm you, plans to give you hope and a future.
Then you will call upon me and come and
pray to me, and I will listen to you. You will
seek me and find me when you seek me with
all your heart. I will be found by you," declares
the LORD, "and will bring you back from
captivity."

—JEREMIAH 29:11–14

You, dear children, are from God and have
overcome them, because the one who is in you
is greater than the one who is in the world.

—1 JOHN 4:4

My children, fear not for this world and be not afraid for
what you would see; how you would see the things of this
world that would change, and the evil that would seek to
consume you and My children, and the things that would
happen—fear not! For surely I tell you that I have a plan
for this world, and though Satan would have his plan and
he would devise his schemes, his plans are as the web of the
spider, they are as the web that you saw this evening: that
though the web would be large and intricate, it would be

before you and it would be real, yet with the movement of your hand, with breath blown from your mouth, this web crumbles—this web is gone! So it is for the plans of Satan, My children, that though he would have the work of his hands, he would look upon it and he would see it as strong and secure, he would think he would be able to live by his plans and his schemes, yet I move My hand, My children, and his web would collapse; yet I blow from My mouth and his plans are taken to the wind and they are lifted high and taken far away. For his plans do not prevail. My plans are victorious. And My children are dear to Me. My children are My loved ones, and I have a plan for this life and for this world, for each of you and for My people in general. And I am specific to you, My children. I speak into your lives. I touch your lives. I guide you and I go with you. Even as this world turns, even as I have a plan for My children in general, yet I have a plan for you—and you are part of the bigger plan. All things are working together, My children. They all come together, and they all come together in Me…in My love…in My plan. So be not afraid and worry not as you see things, for it is as I see things that counts. And as I say, it is My plan that prevails. And what Satan would desire, he has his time, but it is of no consequence; he has his moments, but they do not matter. For it is My time. They are My moments. This is My creation. You are My treasured ones, and I do not let loose of those whom I treasure.

> The thief comes only to steal and kill and destroy; I have come that they may have life, and have it to the full.
>
> —JOHN 10:10

And we know that in all things God works for the good of those who love him, who have been called according to his purpose.

—ROMANS 8:28

———

SPEAK OF FAITH

—During a church service—

"To whom will you compare me? Or who is my equal?" says the Holy One. Lift your eyes and look to the heavens: Who created all these? He who brings out the starry host one by one, and calls them each by name. Because of his great power and mighty strength, not one of them is missing. Why do you say, O Jacob, and complain, O Israel, "my way is hidden from the LORD; my cause is disregarded by my God"? Do you not know? Have you not heard? The LORD is the everlasting God, the Creator of the ends of the earth. He will not grow tired or weary, and his understanding no one can fathom. He gives strength to the weary and increases the power of the weak. Even youths grow tired and weary, and young men stumble and fall; but those who hope in the LORD will renew their strength. They will soar on wings like eagles; they will run and not grow weary, they will walk and not be faint.

—ISAIAH 40:25–31

This is what the LORD says, he who made the earth, the LORD who formed it and established it—the LORD is his name: "Call to me and I will

answer you and tell you great and unsearchable
things you do not know."

—JEREMIAH 33:2–3

My children! You would speak of My creation, and truly I
say to you that I spoke, and the stars took their place in the
heavens; that I spoke, and this world was formed with all
of its life and all of its beauty; by My word, My children—
as I spoke. And I speak now, and I say to you that you are
My children, you are My loved ones, more precious than
all of My creation are you. And I speak into each of your
lives. I speak to you now that there would be faith, for I
am the Lord your God, and I do all things. As I plan, so
it is. As I speak, so it shall be. And I speak now: let there
be faith in your lives. Let there be faith in your hearts, for
there are days to come when I will use you, My children.
I will call you to Me, and you will look upon Me, and the
veils will be lifted—they will be torn apart that you would
see Me and you would know that I am the Lord your God
and I am powerful and I can do all things. Let this be your
faith as this world would come against you. Let this be
your faith as the trial and the sorrows and the heartaches
of this world come: yet I am with you, yet all things I do for
you—as there is faith, My children. As there is faith.

If you do not stand firm in your faith, you will
not stand at all.

—ISAIAH 7:9

But the righteous will live by his faith.

—HABAKKUK 2:4

We live by faith, not by sight.

—2 CORINTHIANS 5:7

———

This Is the Way

—During a prayer meeting—

Commit your way to the LORD; trust in him
and he will do this: He will make your righteousness shine like the dawn, the justice of
your cause like the noonday sun.

—Psalm 37:5–6

Whether you turn to the right or to the left,
your ears will hear a voice behind you, saying,
"This is the way; walk in it."

—Isaiah 30:21

My children, for every day in your life you would see the
sun rise, it would take its place in the sky—you would know
that it is a new day. It is a new day in your life. And My children, you are not alone in this life! You are not alone in this
world! That as you would seek Me, I say to you, it is a new
day in your life—it is a new day with Me and My Spirit. And
I am with you, My children—I am with you. I will go with
you, My children. You will hear My voice. I will call you and
you will hear Me say, "Step this way, My children. This is the
way, walk in it! This is the way, step forward, My children."
It is My voice, for I lead My children, and I call My sheep;
and you are My dear ones, you are My loved ones—for all
things I will do for you. For did I not lay down My life for
you? Did I not give it all for you? And is this not My request
of you, My children? That you also would lay down your
lives for Me and you would give Me your very heart—your
very lives and souls? For it is in this time, My children, that

the fruit will come, and fruit will prosper, and I will prosper you—in Me, My children! Not in the things of this world, but of My Spirit. For it is My Spirit for you. It is My Spirit that you need for the times that are coming and the times that are ahead. It is My Spirit, My children, for all things. And My Spirit is enough, My children. It is enough for you. And I am enough for you. I am enough. This is the way, My children—walk in it! Walk in My Spirit. Walk in My love. Walk in Me, My children. Walk in Me.

> Whoever does not love does not know God, because God is love. This is how God showed his love among us: He sent his one and only Son into the world that we might live through him. This is love: not that we loved God, but that he loved us and sent his Son as an atoning sacrifice for our sins. Dear friends, since God so loved us, we also ought to love one another.
>
> —1 JOHN 4:8–11

> However, as it is written: "No eye has seen, no ear has heard, no mind has conceived what God has prepared for those who love him"– but God has revealed it to us by his Spirit. The Spirit searches all things, even the deep things of God. For who among men knows the thoughts of a man except the man's spirit within him? In the same way no one knows the thoughts of God except the Spirit of God.
>
> —1 CORINTHIANS 2:9–11

> Jesus answered, "I tell you the truth, no one can enter the kingdom of God unless he is born of water and the Spirit. Flesh gives birth to flesh, but the Spirit gives birth to spirit."
>
> —JOHN 3:5–6

⊷⊶

TIME TO SHINE

—During a prayer meeting—

Then the LORD came down in the cloud and stood there with him and proclaimed his name, the LORD. And he passed in front of Moses, proclaiming, "The LORD, the LORD, the compassionate and gracious God, slow to anger, abounding in love and faithfulness, maintaining love to thousands, and forgiving wickedness, rebellion and sin. Yet he does not leave the guilty unpunished; he punishes the children and their children for the sin of the fathers to the third and fourth generation."

—EXODUS 34:5–7

Consecrate yourselves and be holy, because I am the LORD your God. Keep my decrees and follow them. I am the LORD, who makes you holy.

—LEVITICUS 20:7–8

Those whom I love I rebuke and discipline. So be earnest, and repent. Here I am! I stand at the door and knock. If anyone hears my voice and opens the door, I will come in and eat with him, and he with me. To him who overcomes, I will give the right to sit with me on my throne, just as I overcame and sat down with my Father on his throne. He who has an ear, let him hear what the Spirit says to the churches.

—REVELATION 3:19–22

My children, each of you has spoken My name, and since

ancient days My name is unchanging, for My name is the Lord. And I am your God, and you are My children. And to all who seek Me, to all who love Me, I am the Lord. For each of you, My children, I would stand before you and I would knock at the door and you would open the door that I would enter in and I would eat with you. But, My children, in every heart there are many doors and though you would open some, yet there are others that remain closed. There are some that you would not open for the scar is deep. There are others that you yourselves would not know of for they are hidden from you—yet My desire is that every door would be opened, that every room I would live in and My light would shine in your heart. Let this be your prayer, My children, that I would live in you, and that you would live in Me, and that your heart would be pure and holy. For this is My will. And as I am in your heart, so it is that you are holy. You are holy, for I am the Lord who makes you holy. I am the Lord your God. Call on My name. Give Me your heart, My children, for I knock even now. I knock even now for you. I long for you and I will make all things right, that as you would seek Me and give yourselves to Me, it is then that I will use you and you will be a light in this world, a light that will shine. For it is time to shine, My children. It is time to shine. No longer to hide your light. No longer that you would live within the walls of this church. It is time to shine, My children. And you must have My power, you must have My Spirit, you must give Me your heart. Open every door, My children. Open every door. Open it, for it is the Lord who speaks to you. It is the Lord who demands it, My children. I require your hearts. It is time. It is time.

He reveals deep and hidden things; he knows what lies in darkness, and light dwells with him.

—DANIEL 2:22

You are the light of the world. A city on a hill cannot be hidden. Neither do people light a lamp and put it under a bowl. Instead they put it on its stand, and it gives light to everyone in the house. In the same way, let your light shine before men, that they may see your good deeds and praise your Father in heaven.

—MATTHEW 5:14–16

PROMISES

—During a church service—

According to the Lord's own word, we tell you that we who are still alive, who are left till the coming of the Lord, will certainly not precede those who have fallen asleep. For the Lord himself will come down from heaven, with a loud command, with the voice of the archangel and with the trumpet call of God, and the dead in Christ will rise first. After that, we who are still alive and are left will be caught up together with them in the clouds to meet the Lord in the air. And so we will be with the Lord forever.

—1 THESSALONIANS 4:15–17

Do not conform any longer to the pattern of this world, but be transformed by the renewing of your mind. Then you will be able to test and approve what God's will is—his good, pleasing and perfect will.

—ROMANS 12:2

If you obey my commands, you will remain in
my love, just as I have obeyed my Father's commands and remain in his love.

—JOHN 15:10

My children, you would sing of My promises and you
would hold them near to your heart, and I speak to you
again of My promise; that the sun rises each morning, and
though there are those who would lay in the comfort of
their bed and they would wish it not to rise, or there would
be those by their own strength who would try to keep it
from rising, yet every morning the sun rises. And so is My
promise to you, My children: that every day I am with you.
Nothing can stop this, My children. I am with you, and I
would not leave you alone in this world. Those who are
mine, those who would give themselves to Me, surely I will
take you from this place, and you will live with Me. This is
My promise. And let this be your faith, My children—let
it be the very workings of your mind, that each day you
would not conform to this world, but you would be transformed in My Word; that you would read in My Word of
My promises, and you would hold them in your heart,
and you would know My commands and follow them. For
this is your freedom, My children. This is your freedom:
that you would bind yourself to My Word and you would
obey Me. For it is in obedience, My children, that I take
you from this world, and I create a new standard for you
that you would stand apart. Then you are the light, My
children—then the light shines through you, then My joy
is complete in you, then you are transformed and made

new—each morning, My children. Each morning with the sunrise, it is My love that rises in your life and in your heart. In your heart, My children. In your heart.

> We know that we have come to know him if we obey his commands. The man who says, "I know him," but does not do what he commands is a liar, and the truth is not in him. But if anyone obeys his word, God's love is truly made complete in him.
>
> —1 JOHN 2:3–5

> This is how we know that we love the children of God: by loving God and carrying out his commands. This is love for God: to obey his commands. And his commands are not burdensome, for everyone born of God overcomes the world. This is the victory that has overcome the world, even our faith. Who is it that overcomes the world? Only he who believes that Jesus is the Son of God.
>
> —1 JOHN 5:2–5

> Because of the LORD's great love we are not consumed, for his compassions never fail. They are new every morning; great is your faithfulness.
>
> —LAMENTATIONS 3:22–23

> But may they who love you be like the sun when it rises in its strength.
>
> —JUDGES 5:31

———

Grains of Sand

My times are in your hands.

—Psalm 31:15

There is a time for everything, and a season for
every activity under heaven: a time to be born
and a time to die, a time to plant and a time
to uproot, a time to kill and a time to heal, a
time to tear down and a time to build, a time to
weep and a time to laugh, a time to mourn and
a time to dance, a time to scatter stones and
a time to gather them, a time to embrace and
a time to refrain, a time to search and a time
to give up, a time to keep and a time to throw
away, a time to tear and a time to mend, a time
to be silent and a time to speak, a time to love
and a time to hate, a time for war and a time
for peace.

—Ecclesiastes 3:1–8

We give thanks to you, O God, we give thanks,
for your Name is near; men tell of your wonderful deeds. You say, "I choose the appointed
time; it is I who judge uprightly. When the
earth and all its people quake, it is I who hold
its pillars firm."

—Psalm 75:1–3

My children, I see you in your lives, and for you your lives
are measured in time; that the hour glass would stand
before you and for each moment a grain of sand would
fall; you would see it and you would know that another

moment has past. And yet I speak to you now, My children, that you would know that each moment I am with you; with each grain of sand that would fall I see it fall with you and I am with you, My children—at all times…in each moment. And though the sand would fall, yet there is much that remains; much more sand will fall for your lives, My children, as time passes. And even so, in each moment I am still with you. Each moment that is to come, I have seen the sand that will fall; I have chosen each grain, and I know that it will fall and what it will bring for your life—for every moment of your life I have already seen. It has already happened in My eyes, and I have chosen for you what will happen. As you would walk with Me and be obedient to Me, My children, as you would spend time with Me, it is then that the grain that I have chosen falls for your life, and all things happen according to My plan and My purpose. Seek Me, My children. Stay close to Me in your lives, for I am close to you; that every moment, My children, every grain of sand that falls, yet I am with you, My children. I am always with you. Always with you, My children.

> In him we were also chosen, having been predestined according to the plan of him who works out everything in conformity with the purpose of his will, in order that we, who were the first to hope in Christ, might be for the praise of his glory.
>
> —EPHESIANS 1:11–12

> And surely I am with you always, to the very end of the age.
>
> —MATTHEW 28:20

―――•――

MY WAY FOR YOU

―During a prayer meeting―

"For my thoughts are not your thoughts, neither are your ways my ways," declares the LORD. "As the heavens are higher than the earth, so are my ways higher than your ways and my thoughts than your thoughts."

—ISAIAH 55:8–9

Who has known the mind of the Lord? Or who has been his counselor?

—ROMANS 11:34

Now this is what the LORD Almighty says: "Give careful thought to your ways."

—HAGGAI 1:5

…And now I will show you the most excellent way. If I speak in the tongues of men and of angels, but have not love, I am only a resounding gong or a clanging cymbal. If I have the gift of prophecy and can fathom all mysteries and all knowledge, and if I have a faith that can move mountains, but have not love, I am nothing. If I give all I possess to the poor and surrender my body to the flames, but have not love, I gain nothing.

—1 CORINTHIANS 12:31–13:3

My children, you have said the words this evening that your ways are not My ways—it is true, My children! It is right that you would say this, for truly you would see this world, you would look upon My creation, and you would know that it is beyond you. It is beyond your ways—for this world is My way, My children. But even so, I tell you that My ways are your ways, for My ways are for you, My children. My way is truth—it is truth for you, My children. My way is holiness—and you must be holy, My children. My way is the way of love—it is love for you, My children; love must be your way. My ways are your ways, My children, and that is what this life is about. In My creation, in this world, you would learn My ways and you would grow in Me. This is My desire, My children, that My ways would become as your ways because of the love that you would have for Me, because of the desire that you would have for Me, because of the willingness you would have, My children, even as the willingness that I showed you that I went to the cross for you and I died to self. So it is for you, My children, that you must die to self, that you would desire My ways and not your own, My love and not your own, My holiness and not your own, My truth, My children, before the truth of this world. Before the truth of your own mind, it must be My truth. And it is in prayer, My children, and reading of the Word that you would come upon these things and that I would strengthen you and that I would make you as a new person. You would be reborn, My children! Others would look upon you and they would not recognize you because it is My way upon you, My children. It is My way for all things. It is My way I make for you. It is My way that I pave the path, and I call you upon it. Come this way, My children. Come to Me. I have prepared the way. I have spoken of the way. It is the way for you, My children. I am the way. I am the way. Come to Me, My children. I am the way.

Jesus answered, "I am the way and the truth and the life. No one comes to the Father except through me."

—JOHN 14:6

When I was a child, I talked like a child, I thought like a child, I reasoned like a child. When I became a man, I put childish ways behind me. Now we see but a poor reflection as in a mirror; then we shall see face to face. Now I know in part; then I shall know fully, even as I am fully known.

—1 CORINTHIANS 13:11–12

BEGINNING AND END

—During a prayer meeting—

This is what the LORD Almighty says: "In a little while I will once more shake the heavens and the earth, the sea and the dry land. I will shake all nations, and the desired of all nations will come, and I will fill this house with glory," says the LORD Almighty. "The silver is mine and the gold is mine," declares the LORD Almighty. "The glory of this present house will be greater than the glory of the former house," says the LORD Almighty. "And in this place I will grant peace," declares the LORD Almighty.

—HAGGAI 2:6–9

I will repay you for the years the locusts have eaten—the great locust and the young locust, the other locusts and the locust swarm—my great army that I sent among you. You will have plenty to eat, until you are full, and you will praise the name of the LORD your God, who has worked wonders for you; never again will my people be shamed. Then you will know that I am in Israel, that I am the LORD your God, and that there is no other; never again will my people be shamed. And afterward, I will pour out my Spirit on all people. Your sons and daughters will prophesy, your old men will dream dreams, your young men will see visions. Even on my servants, both men and women, I will pour out my Spirit in those days. I will show wonders in the heavens and on the earth, blood and fire and billows of smoke. The sun will be turned to darkness and the moon to blood before the coming of the great and dreadful day of the LORD. And everyone who calls on the name of the LORD will be saved; for on Mount Zion and in Jerusalem there will be deliverance, as the LORD has said, among the survivors whom the LORD calls.

—JOEL 2:25–32

I am the Alpha and the Omega, the First and the Last, the Beginning and the End.

—REVELATION 22:13

My children! I speak truth to you, My children! That for every age of this world, that there is a beginning and an end; for every age of man there is a start and there is a finish. And for this age, My children, you would see that as it began, in the beginning, My children, that it would be as you who would look upon the sun as it would rise in the sky, it would be the glory of the sunrise, My children. There would be warmth and there would be glory in the clouds, and your eyes would see, and you would believe, and you would know. It was the beginning, My children, but now is the time that the sun would be high above you, and each day is the same, and the sun would take your strength from you, and you would long for the glory—you would long for the rising sun; yet it is as a picture that you could see in your mind—but you do not live it! I tell you now, My children, I have seen the beginning, and I have seen the end. I have seen what is the past, and I see what awaits you, My children. For you, My children, it is the setting of the sun—it is the end of the age. And there is more glory in the setting than in the rising, My children; there is more glory ahead than what has been. I tell you now, that again you will see My glory in the clouds. You will see the light of My love, and you will see the power—and I will give you the power, My children. That as the wind would blow, yet you would direct its path; yet the wind would blow as you would command. You would steer the wind, My children—for it would be My Spirit. And as you would gather and as you would pray, even as you pray now, I will release My Spirit. You will see, My children, the glory of the end… the glory of the end, for it is coming, My children. It is almost upon you! It is the glory, My children! Have faith! Fear not! Be strong! These are My words, My children. These are My words to you.

> At that time men will see the Son of Man coming in clouds with great power and glory.
>
> —MARK 13:26

> Again the high priest asked him, "Are you the Christ, the Son of the Blessed One?" "I am," said Jesus. "And you will see the Son of Man sitting at the right hand of the Mighty One and coming on the clouds of heaven."
>
> —MARK 14:61–62

He is coming with the clouds, and every eye will see him, even those who pierced him; and all the peoples of the earth will mourn because of him. So shall it be! Amen. "I am the Alpha and the Omega," says the Lord God, "who is, and who was, and who is to come, the Almighty."

—Revelation 1:7–8

The End Times

—During a prayer meeting—

You will hear of wars and rumors of wars, but see to it that you are not alarmed. Such things must happen, but the end is still to come. Nation will rise against nation, and kingdom against kingdom. There will be famines and earthquakes in various places. All these are the beginning of birth pains.

—Matthew 24:6–8

No one knows about that day or hour, not even the angels in heaven, nor the Son, but only the Father.

—Mark 13:32

If my people, who are called by my name, will humble themselves and pray and seek my face and turn from their wicked ways, then will I hear from heaven and will forgive their sin and will heal their land. Now my eyes will be open and my ears attentive to the prayers offered in this place.

—2 Chronicles 7:14–15

My children, you would lift your faces and you would look to the stars; and you would see the stars, My children, and would know that though you would reach with your hands yet you cannot touch the stars, for there is a great distance between you and the stars. Not in your lifetime will you touch the stars with your hands. And so it is for many, My children, that they would read My Word and they would read of wars and rumors of wars, they would read of the birth pains, and they would think to themselves, "Not in my lifetime. Not in my lifetime." And yet I say to you, no one knows the time, My children. No one knows the hour. Only I know. And each moment should be lived as if the hour were at hand. This is the time, My children, that My Spirit would be free, that My Spirit would live in you, and that you would seek Me with all your heart, My children; with every part of your being let it be My eyes that you would seek, let it be My face that you would seek. For I tell you, My children, this is the hour that as you seek Me, you will find Me, My children; this is the hour that as you would pray, yet I hear your prayers and I respond, My children. This is the hour in your lives that you would pray for your loved ones, you would pray for your children, and you would pray for this church and this nation. This is the hour, My children, that you would humble yourselves before Me and you would pray, for it is My desire to lift this nation, it is My desire to reveal myself in your hearts, in your lives, in this nation. And yet it will not be unless there is prayer, unless this church would unite and seek Me. And this is My desire—let it be your desire as well, My children; let it be the hunger of your heart that My name would be glorified. This is My desire—let it be your desire, let it be your prayers. For you do not know the hour. You do not know the time. You do not know the hour in which you live.

For my house will be called a house of prayer for all nations.

—ISAIAH 56:7

"I tell you the truth, whatever you bind on earth will be bound in heaven, and whatever you loose on earth will be loosed in heaven. Again, I tell you that if two of you on earth agree about anything you ask for, it will be done for you by my Father in heaven. For where two or three come together in my name, there am I with them."

—MATTHEW 18:18–20

For the eyes of the LORD range throughout the earth to strengthen those whose hearts are fully committed to him.

—2 CHRONICLES 16:9

Make every effort to keep the unity of the Spirit through the bond of peace. There is one body and one Spirit—just as you were called to one hope when you were called—one Lord, one faith, one baptism; one God and Father of all, who is over all and through all and in all.

—EPHESIANS 4:3–6

May the God who gives endurance and encouragement give you a spirit of unity among yourselves as you follow Christ Jesus, so that with one heart and mouth you may glorify the God and Father of our Lord Jesus Christ.

—ROMANS 15:5–6

GIVE TO ME WHAT IS MINE

—During a church service after a sermon on tithing—

He does not take his eyes off the righteous; he enthrones them with kings and exalts them forever.

—JOB 36:7

O great and powerful God, whose name is the LORD Almighty, great are your purposes and mighty are your deeds. Your eyes are open to all the ways of men; you reward everyone according to his conduct and as his deeds deserve.

—JEREMIAH 32:18–20

My children! My dear ones! I see you in this life, I see you in this world, and always, My children, My eyes are upon you. My eyes do not close in sleep; they are not distracted from you in your lives, My children, and always My eyes are filled with love, always I speak to you in the love of My heart. And these are My words to you, My children, these are My words to you: that the wealth of this world does not compare to that which I can give to you. The wealth that you would hold in your hands does not compare to the wealth of My love and to My Spirit. And truly, My love moves as I command, and My Spirit flows where I desire. Open wide the windows of your mind, open wide the doorways to your heart that My love would flow in, that My Spirit would flow in, and that I would change you, My children, into My image—as I desire. These are My words, My children: that I will prosper you in the Spirit. I will prosper you in My love. I will give to you beyond what you know, beyond what you can have in this world. These are My words, My children: give to Me that which is Mine! Give to Me of your time. Give to Me of your love. That you would read the Bible, that you would spend time in prayer, and that you would give to this church of the wealth that I would give you. These are My words, My children, they are yours to claim, they are yours to put aside, it is yours to decide, My children. Even so, they are My words.

"I the LORD do not change. So you, O descendants of Jacob, are not destroyed. Ever since the time of your forefathers you have turned away from my decrees and have not kept them. Return to me, and I will return to you," says the LORD Almighty. "But you ask, 'How are we to return?' Will a man rob God? Yet you rob me. But you ask, 'How do we rob you?' In tithes and offerings. You are under a curse—the whole nation of you—because you are robbing me. Bring the whole tithe into the storehouse, that there may be food in my house. Test me in this," says the LORD Almighty, "and see if I will not throw open the floodgates of heaven and pour out so much blessing that you will not have room enough for it. I will prevent pests from devouring your crops, and the vines in your fields will not cast their fruit," says the LORD Almighty. "Then all the nations will call you blessed, for yours will be a delightful land," says the LORD Almighty.

—MALACHI 3:6–12

I AM IN YOUR HOUSE

—During a church service—

They will build houses and dwell in them.

—ISAIAH 65:21

Unless the LORD builds the house, its builders
labor in vain.

—PSALM 127:1

The LORD's curse is on the house of the wicked,
but he blesses the home of the righteous.

—PROVERBS 3:33

My children! My dear ones! I would give you the land, and
you would build the house, and the house is as your life
that to those who would pass by, those who would look
upon it, all would seem well: your lawn is manicured, the
house is painted, the light shines in the window—and all
is well. And yet I see into your life, and I tell you now, you
are not alone in your life! For truly, I see your thoughts.
Truly, I know your needs, that as this world would seek
to consume you, as the trial and sorrow would come
upon you, yet I am with you, yet I am in your house, My
children. And it is My desire that I would take your fire
and I would renew it, and what was cold would be made
warm, and what was dark would be made light that your
light would shine forth, and what people would see as
they pass by would be My glory, My children. This is My
desire: that you would seek after Me, that all that you
have you would give to Me. For it is then, My children,
that you will find Me. It is then that all I have I give to
you, it is then that your house is in order—and it is beautiful, My children…it is warm, and you will invite others
into your house and they will see Me. This is My desire,
My children, be encouraged in your life for I am with
you; love Me for I love you, and if I love you who can be
against you, My children? What harm can become you?
Seek after Me, I say—for I love you dearly. Seek after Me,

for all that I have I give to you.

> Jesus replied, "If anyone loves me, he will obey my teaching. My Father will love him, and we will come to him and make our home with him."
>
> —John 14:23

> "And I will fill this house with glory," says the Lord Almighty.
>
> —Haggai 2:7

> What, then, shall we say in response to this? If God is for us, who can be against us?
>
> —Romans 8:31

Freedom for You

—During a prayer meeting—

> To the Jews who had believed him, Jesus said, "If you hold to my teaching, you are really my disciples. Then you will know the truth, and the truth will set you free."
>
> —John 8:31–32

> Above all, love each other deeply, because love covers over a multitude of sins.
>
> —1 Peter 4:8

> What shall we say, then? Is the law sin? Certainly not! Indeed I would not have known what sin was except through the law.
>
> —Romans 7:7

My children, you would speak of your freedom and you would pray for the liberty, and I speak truth to you now,

My children, that in My Word there is perfect liberty. In My Word there is complete freedom. For those who would know My Word, for those who would follow My teaching, these are truly My disciples, and it is then that the truth is known, and it is then that there is freedom, My children. There is freedom for you, that My Word and My teachings are not as a prison; they are not as a weight that you would carry that would drive you to the ground. For My Word and My teaching bring freedom. For My Word is based solely in love, My children. Does not love cover all sins? And in love, would it not keep you from sinning, that as you would love Me completely and you would understand the Word, would you not stay away from the sin that would seek to consume you? The sin that would shield you from Me and Me from you? It is My desire that every barrier would be laid low between us and every veil be torn wide open—and this can be, My children—as you will study My Word, as you will place it in your heart, as you will ask for the revelation and how it will apply to you, and as you will know that even when you fall short, even when you knowingly sin, still My love covers your sin, still the cross is before you, still I died—and yet I rose! Still, My children, you are forgiven, for I love you dearly. Seek after Me. Press into Me. Let your prayer life expand—let it be the most important part of your life, that you would speak to Me, and I would speak to you, and I would teach you of Me, and you would know yourself, My children. For it is then that you would have the answers—is this sin? Does not My Spirit convict? Does not My Spirit lead? And yet, does not My Spirit set you free? Even as you have read tonight, even as you have prayed, even as it has been spoken, this is truth: that in My Spirit there is liberty, and there is freedom—and it is for you, My children! It all is for you…it awaits you…it is before you now. O that you would grasp it! O that you would hold onto it! For I give it to you. My children, these words I place in your mind; only you can bring them to your heart. Take them into your heart, My children, and cherish them, and understand that I am for you—I am always for you. In Me there is freedom because in Me there is perfect love—and it is for you My children, it's always for you.

> Now the Lord is the Spirit, and where the Spirit of the Lord is, there is freedom.
> —2 CORINTHIANS 3:17

> And so we know and rely on the love God has for us. God is love. Whoever lives in love lives in God, and God in him.
> —1 JOHN 4:16

THE WIND

—During a prayer meeting attended by several people
that did not believe in spiritual gifts—

> You should not be surprised at my saying, "You must be born again." The wind blows wherever it pleases. You hear its sound, but you cannot tell where it comes from or where it is going. So it is with everyone born of the Spirit.
> —JOHN 3:7–8

My children, there are those among you who would come to the mountain and you would stand in the meadow to see the mountain: to see its beauty, to see its strength, to know that it is the mountain and that the mountain does not change. And you would stand in the meadow, and you would see all that is beautiful: you would see the flowers that would grow, you would see the trees—tall from their roots that would stand in the soil. You would take it all in, My children, and in the midst of what you would see, yet the wind would blow, and you would see the wind and how it would blow the trees and how it would blow the grass of the meadow. And for some, there is confusion in the wind, My children. The wind would come, and it would disturb your thoughts, and it would distract your view—for you have come to see the mountain. You did not expect the wind. You would not know what the wind is, for truly the wind has not blown upon you in your lives. These are My words to you, My children: let the wind be as My Spirit. Do not be distracted. Do not be confused. For if you would see the mountain, if you would live the life in the meadow, yet the wind will blow, My children. The wind is part of the experience, for the wind is part of Me. Receive My Spirit! Do not be confused! Do not say, "This is not for me. I accept the mountain, I will not accept the wind." The wind is for you, My children, because I am for you. If you would receive Me, you must receive all of Me. It is not a part of Me, My children—it is all of Me. For I am for you—I am in you, and you are in Me. These are My words, My children. These are My words.

> May the grace of the Lord Jesus Christ, and the love of God, and the fellowship of the Holy Spirit be with you all.
>
> —2 Corinthians 13:14

> If you love me, you will obey what I command. And I will ask the Father, and he will give you

another Counselor to be with you forever—the Spirit of truth. The world cannot accept him, because it neither sees him nor knows him. But you know him, for he lives with you and will be in you. I will not leave you as orphans; I will come to you.

—JOHN 14:15–18

—◈—

NEW BIRTH

—During a church service—

Jesus answered, "I tell you the truth, no one can enter the kingdom of God unless he is born of water and the Spirit. Flesh gives birth to flesh, but the Spirit gives birth to spirit."

—JOHN 3:5–6

He chose to give us birth through the word of truth, that we might be a kind of firstfruits of all he created.

—JAMES 1:18

Praise be to the God and Father of our Lord Jesus Christ! In his great mercy he has given us new birth into a living hope through the resurrection of Jesus Christ from the dead, and into an inheritance that can never perish, spoil or fade—kept in heaven for you, who through faith are shielded by God's power until the coming of the salvation that is ready to be revealed in the last time.

—1 PETER 1:3–5

My Children! These are My words, My children—these

are My words to you: that truly I am the beginning of all things, that truly birth in Me is as moving from death to life. For there is birth of the flesh, and there is birth in the spirit—and more precious is the birth of the spirit, My children; more precious is My life that would live within you. And these are My words to you: that there are those who would hear this voice who have not yet received me; there are those who have confessed Me with their lips and yet have not known Me in their hearts—in your hearts, My children! This is My desire: that there would be life. This is My desire: that there would be a new birth within you, that you would place aside the sin that hinders you, that you would open your hearts, and that truly you would live, that truly there would be life, that truly you would be reborn—it is in Me, My children. It is all in Me. It is the passion of your heart, that you would give it to Me. It is the desire of every thought, that you would focus on Me. It is all for Me, My children—and in Me there is only life. It is life for you, as you desire, as you choose—as you choose Me.

> Therefore, since we are surrounded by such a great cloud of witnesses, let us throw off everything that hinders and the sin that so easily entangles, and let us run with perseverance the race marked out for us.
>
> —HEBREWS 12:1

> We demolish arguments and every pretension that sets itself up against the knowledge of God, and we take captive every thought to make it obedient to Christ.
>
> —2 CORINTHIANS 10:5

Yet if you devote your heart to him and stretch out your hands to him, if you put away the sin that is in your hand and allow no evil to dwell in your tent, then you will lift up your face without shame; you will stand firm and without fear. You will surely forget your trouble, recalling it only as waters gone by. Life will be brighter than midday, and darkness will become like morning. You will be secure, because there is hope; you will look about you and take your rest in safety. You will lie down, with no one to make you afraid, and many will court your favor.

—JOB 11:13–19

DRINK OF THE CUP

—During a prayer meeting—

He took Peter, James, and John along with him, and he began to be deeply distressed and troubled. "My soul is overwhelmed with sorrow to the point of death," he said to them. "Stay here and keep watch." Going a little farther, he fell to the ground and prayed that if possible the hour might pass from him. "Abba, Father," he said, "everything is possible for you. Take this cup from me. Yet not what I will, but what you will."

—MARK 14:33–36

This, then, is how you should pray: "Our Father in heaven, hallowed be your name, your kingdom come, your will be done on earth as it is in heaven."

—MATTHEW 6:9–10

My children, you are in My presence now, and I am with you. Do not think that I would only know you from afar. Do not think that I would hold you away from Me. For I am with you, My children, and I know your every need, and I know your desires. I speak to you of a time when I was in need and I had desires, for I knelt in the garden and the despair of My life was upon Me. The cup from which I would drink was upon Me and, O that it would be put aside, O that I would not drink of that cup! For I knew what was coming, and I knew what would be. My children, I have felt the emotions that you would feel, I have had longings, and always My desire was for the Father—always My desire was for His will. And so it must be for you, My children. Know that I understand you. Know that I see your desires and, even so, let your desire be for the Father! Let your desire be for His will. Drink of the cup, My children. Drink of the cup that I place before you. Drink of the cup, for even as I endured the cross, yet I had the victory. Even as I endured the pain and the suffering, yet I saw you and it was all worth it, My children, it was worth it that I would know your love; it was worth it that you would know Mine. This was the task that was before Me, and it is the task that is before you, that you would know My love and that you would give your love to Me. Know this, My children: I am your Father and I love you as a Father. Let your will be for Me and your desire be for Me and, I will strengthen you in this life. I will help you. You will know My love. And the coldness of this world, My children, I will protect you from it. Even as at this time you would sit in this house and you would feel the warmth about you and the comfort—yet outside it is cold, so it shall be in your lives that My hand will be all about you, and I will protect you, and you will know warmth and love. Even as the world is cold, even as the cold would tear you down, yet I will build you up. Know this, My children. Let it be your faith. Let it be your desire. Let it be your will. For it is My will, My children. And you are My desire. You are My desire.

> Let us fix our eyes on Jesus, the author and perfecter of our faith, who for the joy set before him endured the cross, scorning its shame, and sat down at the right hand of the throne of God.
>
> —HEBREWS 12:2

> Then Jesus said to his disciples, "If anyone would come after me, he must deny himself and take up his cross and follow me. For whoever wants to save his life will lose it, but whoever loses his life for me will find it. What good will it be for a man if he gains the whole world, yet forfeits his soul? Or what can a man give in exchange for his soul?
>
> —MATTHEW 16:24–26

> Therefore let everyone who is godly pray to you while you may be found; surely when the mighty waters rise, they will not reach him. You are my hiding place; you will protect me from trouble and surround me with songs of deliverance.
>
> —PSALM 32:6–7

CHAPTER 9

THE GREAT COMMISSION

Then Jesus came to them and said, "All authority under heaven and earth has been given to me. Therefore, go and make disciples of all nations, baptizing them in the name of the Father and the Son and of the Holy Spirit, and teaching then to obey everything I have commanded you. And surely I will be with you always, to the very end of the age."

—MATTHEW 28:18–20

As amazing and truly magnificent as our God is, His purposes and plans are simple and consistent in nature: to draw all of mankind to Him. For those who know Him, it is that we would know Him in greater depth, understanding, and love. For those who do not know Him, His burning desire, the yearning of His heart, is that they would come to Him and accept Him as their Lord. Whether we accept Him or not, He is Lord. Every knee will bow before Him and every tongue confess the name of Jesus. The decisions we make and what we will or will not believe do not change who God is. Those who do not receive Jesus as their own will be lost forever, and it is the terrible all-consuming desire of our Father that none would perish.

Our Father wants each person, each of His lost sheep, to find his way to Him so that He can save him. And it breaks His heart that there are those who will not receive what has already been freely and lovingly given. Sorrow upon sorrow for our Lord that He must send those who will not call upon Jesus away from Him for all eternity.

Our Good Shepherd wants us to know His heart, and His heart is for His lost sheep. Our Father loves those who are lost even as He loves those who are saved—and His love is far beyond anything we can know. If we truly love the Lord and if we are truly obedient to His calling, there is no stepping back from an active and passionate desire to be used of the Holy Spirit to bring the lost home to Christ. As we spend time with the Lord in prayer, and as we read the Holy Bible, He will help us keep our eyes focused on things that are of Him, things that are everlasting, and there is nothing more important to the Lord than the eternal destiny of His dear children. There is no denying this truth, and that this, too, is another area where the Lord wants to see His church awakened. Beyond being occupied with the problems of our own lives, the Lord wants us to see the eternal loss to heaven and to Him that happens when one of His dear and precious children is turned away from Him because he did not accept Jesus. Beyond dwelling on our own concerns, our Lord wants us to be obedient to the commission He has placed on His church and the call He has placed on our lives.

While we may accept the commission and seek to move forward in our calling, our efforts are fruitless unless we receive the fullness of His glory through the power of the Holy Spirit living in us. Our walking in the fullness of

Christ and the weapons given us to defeat Satan are the same: God's Holy Spirit, His Holy Word, the blood of the Lamb, and the testimony of our faith. We must be filled with the Holy Spirit and walk in obedience with the Lord, and our loving Father will fill us with boldness and put words in our own mouths to lead the lost home to Him. We must know the Lord's ways and His promises and His truths. We will receive this understanding through the Holy Bible and through seeking the Lord in prayer and in fasting. We must believe in our hearts that through our faith in the cross of Jesus Christ we are redeemed from each and every sin our lives. Our lives and experiences must become a testimony that is freely shared, not out of obligation to our Lord, but because we have seen Him, because we know and love Him, and because He has done great and mighty things in our lives. Within these we will grow in the Lord, and against these Satan cannot stand.

The Word of God and the testimony of Jesus Christ must be a living word coming forth in our lives anointed by the power of the Holy Spirit. Truly, as we seek the Lord in all things, the Word of God and the testimony of Jesus will become our very lives. The Lord wants to fill us with His own perfect love, so that we in turn will love others perfectly and light the way for the salvation of their souls. It is for our love for our Father and His love for the lost. Since our Lord Jesus paid such a high price for our lives, can we do anything other than respond to His call? Since the Father Himself asks us, can we say anything other than *yes?* Let the lost be found, O Lord. Let the commission be fulfilled for your own sake!

—◆—

FIND MY LOST CHILDREN

—One of four prophetic moves by the Holy Spirit during a church service
when the Lord was encouraging the congregation to be strong in Him—

When I consider your heavens, the work of
your fingers, the moon and the stars, which
you have set in place, what is man that you are
mindful of him, the son of man that you care
for him?

—PSALM 8:3–4

He determines the number of the stars and
calls them each by name.

—PSALM 147:4

You answer us with awesome deeds of righteousness, O God our Savior, the hope of all the
ends of the earth and of the farthest seas, who
formed the mountains by your power, having
armed yourself with strength, who stilled the
roaring of the seas, the roaring of their waves,
and the turmoil of the nations. Those living far
away fear your wonders; where morning dawns
and evening fades you call forth songs of joy.

—PSALM 65:5–8

My children, I speak to you now, and I would say to you:
point to the star in the heavens, and I will tell you the distance from the tip of your finger to that star, for I placed the
star in the heavens. And point to the rock of the mountain,
and I will tell you the very age of the rock, for I formed it
with My own hands. And point to the bird in the air as it
would fly, and I will speak to you of the design of its wings

and its feathers, for it is the creation of My own mind. All of this is My creation, and I love it dearly—and yet I love you more. I have called you apart, and I would call you My children, and I would seek to pour My love into you. You would ask to know Me and to know Me more, and so I share with you now, I share with you My own burden, the burden of My heart, that there are other children whom I love equally as you, and yet they do not know Me. And every moment of every day, their lives would end in this world—they would pass on without knowing Me. And, O that the world was as they had thought. O that their lives were truly over. For they will not see Me for all of eternity. This is My burden. And you are My children, so I share My burden with you. I place this burden on you as well. And I say to you, find My lost sheep. Find My lost children. But be not afraid, for already I have picked up the shield of love in My left hand and the sword of righteousness in My right, and with love and grace in My heart I will go before you. I will clear the path. I will prepare the way. And the battle has already been won. I am already victorious. I only ask that you be ready, that you seek Me, and that you find My lost children. Find My lost children.

> Once more Jesus said to them, "I am going away, and you will look for me, and you will die in your sin. Where I go, you cannot come."
> —JOHN 8:21

> The LORD will fight for you; you need only to be still.
> —EXODUS 14:14

> For I have come down from heaven not to do my will but to do the will of him who sent me.

And this is the will of him who sent me, that I shall lose none of all that he has given me, but raise them up at the last day. For my Father's will is that everyone who looks to the Son and believes in him shall have eternal life, and I will raise him up at the last day.

—JOHN 6:38–40

MY FAITHFULNESS

—During a church service—

Know therefore that the LORD your God is God; he is the faithful God, keeping his covenant of love to a thousand generations of those who love him and keep his commands.

—DEUTERONOMY 7:9

I am the LORD, and there is no other; apart from me there is no God. I will strengthen you, though you have not acknowledged me, so that from the rising of the sun to the place of its setting men may know there is none besides me. I am the LORD, and there is no other. I form the light and create darkness, I bring prosperity and create disaster; I, the LORD, do all these things.

—ISAIAH 45:5–7

I am the Lord, and I am your God. And I would ask you now to consider My creation— to consider the sun. In all of My creation, is there anything more faithful? Is there anything more true? That every morning the sun would rise and it would move across the sky, and every evening it would set. This is true every day. Since the beginning of creation this has happened. And yet the sun is My creation, and the one who created the sun is more faithful and is more true to His children. And so I say to you, every day it is My love that shines upon you. Every day, it is My power with which I seek to fill you. And every day, as you would look upon the sun, let it be as a remembrance of me, that you would know that I am with you, that you would know that My love rests upon you, and that you would take this remembrance and it would cause you to seek out My lost children, to find My lost children, to seek Me in your hearts, that you would pray to Me. Pray for My Spirit and My anointing and surely I will fill you with My Spirit. Surely you will be anointed that you would go forth into the world with boldness and with strength. For this is My will for you. This is My will.

> In the same way your Father in heaven is not willing that any of these little ones should be lost.
>
> —MATTHEW 18:14

> If you then, though you are evil, know how to give good gifts to your children, how much more will your Father in heaven give the Holy Spirit to those who ask him!
>
> —LUKE 11:13

> When the Counselor comes, whom I will send to you from the Father, the Spirit of truth who goes out from the Father, he will testify about me. And you also must testify, for you have been with me from the beginning.
>
> —JOHN 15:26–27

> When he comes, he will convict the world of guilt in regard to sin and righteousness and judgment: in regard to sin, because men do

not believe in me; in regard to righteousness, because I am going to the Father, where you can see me no longer; and in regard to judgment, because the prince of this world now stands condemned. "I have much more to say to you, more than you can now bear. But when he, the Spirit of truth, comes, he will guide you into all truth. He will not speak on his own; he will speak only what he hears, and he will tell you what is yet to come. He will bring glory to me by taking from what is mine and making it known to you. All that belongs to the Father is mine. That is why I said the Spirit will take from what is mine and make it known to you.

—JOHN 16:8–15

YOUR OBEDIENCE

—During a church service requesting the congregation's support for a major fundraising program—

But I am a worm and not a man, scorned by men and despised by the people. All who see me mock me; they hurl insults, shaking their heads: "He trusts in the LORD; let the LORD rescue him. Let him deliver him, since he delights in him."

—PSALM 22:6–8

Jesus said to them, "Surely you will quote this proverb to me: 'Physician, heal yourself!'"

—LUKE 4:23

For I have come down from heaven not to do my will but to do the will of him who sent me.

—JOHN 6:37

My children, I speak to you of a time in My own life when I was high and lifted up; it was not in glory and authority as you would sing of. Instead I was high and lifted; My body was bruised and battered and pierced and bloodied. Many looked upon me; they spoke of Me and mocked Me. "He has saved others—let him save himself." They would say this with a shred of hope, and yet they would be shrouded in doubt. The doubt would overwhelm the hope, for though they would desire their Savior…their Messiah, yet they saw the carpenter. They saw the man who spoke and confused and baffled, and as they looked upon Me they could not know that only hours before yet I myself prayed that I would not be placed upon the cross, that I would be spared that cup. With great despair and agony I pleaded with the Father that not My own will, but His will be done. And so it was that the cup was held to My lips, and I was asked to drink. So it was, that I drank from this cup in obedience and love for My Father—and love for all. For everything I did, I did for the Father, according to His plan, according to His purpose and His desire—not My own. And so it should be for you, My children, that you would follow this example. Though I was given the power and the authority that none would have placed Me upon the cross, none would have spit on My face or smashed My face with their fists, yet I allowed it to happen—for it was the Father's will. You must seek out the Father's will for your life. You must be obedient to that call. This is My call to you now, My children: that there would be obedience, that you would seek Me with all of your heart, that you would invest of your time and your mind and your heart for Me. For as you do, it is then that I will speak to you, it is then that you will know the desires of My heart for you—what it is that I would have you do. There must be obedience, My children, that you would put your own desires, your own plans aside; you would step forward in faith; you would step forward in unity in this church. From here, My children, I will bless you. As you reach this place of obedience and unity I will choose to let My Spirit flow freely upon you. For this is not a battle of the flesh, neither is it truly a battle of finances for this church, this is a battle of the spirit; and as you overcome your own pride and selfishness, as you submit to the Father and His will, in the spirit you will be set free; in the spirit you will be built up and strengthened. It is then that I will use you for the glory of the Father. It is then that you will be used mightily for the gospel. The word of God and the testimony of Jesus Christ would come from this church and spread through this valley that My name would be lifted high and people would see Me as their Lord and as their God. This is My desire. This is My desire for this church. This is My desire for this time and for this people. And as I desire so it shall be, My children. So it shall be.

> "My food," said Jesus, "is to do the will of him who sent me and to finish his work."
>
> —JOHN 4:34

> But Samuel replied: "Does the LORD delight in burnt offerings and sacrifices as much as in obeying the voice of the LORD? To obey is better than sacrifice, and to heed is better than the fat of rams."
>
> —1 SAMUEL 15:22

Finally, be strong in the Lord and in his mighty power. Put on the full armor of God so that you can take your stand against the devil's schemes. For our struggle is not against flesh and blood, but against the rulers, against the authorities, against the powers of this dark world and against the spiritual forces of evil in the heavenly realms. Therefore put on the full armor of God, so that when the day of evil comes, you may be able to stand your ground, and after you have done everything, to stand.

—Ephesians 6:10–13

But the plans of the Lord stand firm forever, the purposes of his heart through all generations.

—Psalm 33:11

Turn From Your Ways!

—During a church meeting, after a discussion about abortion—

In God, whose word I praise, in the Lord, whose word I praise—in God I trust; I will not be afraid. What can man do to me?

—Psalm 56:10–11

As it is written: "There is no one righteous, not even one; there is no one who understands, no one who seeks God. All have turned away, they have together become worthless; there is no one who does good, not even one."

—Romans 3:10–12

You slaughtered my children and sacrificed them to the idols.

—Ezekiel 16:21

> They have built the high places of Topheth in
> the Valley of Ben Hinnom to burn their sons
> and daughters in the fire—something I did not
> command, nor did it enter my mind.
>
> —JEREMIAH 7:31

I am the Lord, and I am your God. And I would speak to you now of this nation; I would speak to you now of this time. For on your currency you would have the phrase, "In God We Trust." And yet I would ask you, to whom do you refer? Which god do you trust? For do you even know My name? Do you know Me as God? For is there not an evilness upon this nation? Have you not turned away from Me? Even in My chosen people, as they turned from Me, was there not judgment upon them? Did I not judge them? As they would take their children and sacrifice them to other gods, was this not appalling to Me? And did I not bring My judgment? And yet in this day, in this nation, you would sacrifice My children, but not to other gods—for yourselves! For your convenience! For your lifestyle! This cannot be, My children! You cannot continue in this way without My judgment. And so I say to you now, Repent! Repent! And know now that every moment of every day, yet My people's lives would end, they would leave this world, they would come to Me, and yet I must tell them, away from Me! Away from Me, for I never knew you! Away from Me, for there is evil in your heart and though I spoke to you, you did not hear! Though I called you, you would not come. And so this is My call to you now, My children, that you would know, that from the day the word was spoken to this very moment and on until the end of this age, I am the stone that would make

142

you stumble and the rock that would make you fall. And I stand before you now and I say to you: turn from your ways! Turn from your ways and seek Me! Let there be prayer amongst you. Let there be fasting for this nation. For you have heard the condition, you have heard the pending judgment. And yet I call upon you now. I call upon you to seek My grace, to seek My mercy, to pray for this nation that they would turn from their sins, they would turn to the light, and they would turn to My love. For My love is still here. My love is here. And so it is, My children, the mouth of the Lord has spoken.

> Then I will tell them plainly, "I never knew you. Away from me, you evildoers!" Therefore everyone who hears these words of mine and puts them into practice is like a wise man who built his house on the rock. The rain came down, the streams rose, and the winds blew and beat against that house; yet it did not fall, because it had its foundation on the rock. But everyone who hears these words of mine and does not put them into practice is like a foolish man who built his house on sand. The rain came down, the streams rose, and the winds blew and beat against that house, and it fell with a great crash.
>
> —MATTHEW 7:23–27

> And he will be a sanctuary; but for both houses of Israel he will be a stone that causes men to stumble and a rock that makes them fall. And for the people of Jerusalem he will be a trap and a snare.
>
> —ISAIAH 8:14

> "He must turn from evil and do good; he must

seek peace and pursue it. For the eyes of the LORD are on the righteous and his ears are attentive to their prayer, but the face of the LORD is against those who do evil."

—1 PETER 3:11–12

May he turn our hearts to him, to walk in all his ways and to keep the commands, decrees and regulations he gave our fathers.

—1 KINGS 8:58

Have mercy on me, O God, according to your unfailing love; according to your great compassion blot out my transgressions. Wash away all my iniquity and cleanse me from my sin. For I know my transgressions, and my sin is always before me. Against you, you only, have I sinned and done what is evil in your sight, so that you are proved right when you speak and justified when you judge. Surely I was sinful at birth, sinful from the time my mother conceived me. Surely you desire truth in the inner parts; you teach me wisdom in the inmost place. Cleanse me with hyssop, and I will be clean; wash me, and I will be whiter than snow. Let me hear joy and gladness; let the bones you have crushed rejoice. Hide your face from my sins and blot out all my iniquity. Create in me a pure heart, O God, and renew a steadfast spirit within me. Do not cast me from your presence or take your Holy Spirit from me. Restore to me the joy of your salvation and grant me a willing spirit, to sustain me. Then I will teach transgressors your ways, and sinners will turn back to you. Save me from bloodguilt, O God, the God who saves me, and my tongue will sing of your righteousness. O Lord, open my lips, and my mouth will declare your praise. You do not delight in sacrifice, or I would bring it;

you do not take pleasure in burnt offerings. The sacrifices of God are a broken spirit; a broken and contrite heart, O God, you will not despise. In your good pleasure make Zion prosper; build up the walls of Jerusalem. Then there will be righteous sacrifices, whole burnt offerings to delight you; then bulls will be offered on your altar.

—PSALM 51:1–19

RETURN TO ME

—During a church service—

He said, "Go and tell this people: 'Be ever hearing, but never understanding; be ever seeing, but never perceiving. Make the heart of this people calloused; make their ears dull and close their eyes. Otherwise they might see with their eyes, hear with their ears, understand with their hearts, and turn and be healed.'"

—ISAIAH 6:9–10

I am the Lord, and I am your God; I am the living God—I am the Lord who heals you. And I speak that you would hear and you would understand. I stand before you that you would open your eyes and you would see Me. I stretch forth My hand that I would touch your heart, and your heart would soften and you would be healed. Return to Me, My children. Return to Me. For even now I speak your name. I call you, My children, that you would return and you would come to me; that you would seek Me in your prayers, and you would give your lives to Me. For in that time, My children, I will live in your heart, I will live

145

in your thoughts—I will be your life. And I will fill you with boldness and My Spirit. And I will put words in your mouth. And you will stand before My lost sheep and these will be your words: He is My Lord. He is My God. He is the Living God. He is the Lord who has healed Me.

> "This is the covenant I will make with the house of Israel after that time," declares the LORD. "I will put my law in their minds and write it on their hearts. I will be their God, and they will be my people. No longer will a man teach his neighbor, or a man his brother, saying, 'Know the LORD,' because they will all know me, from the least of them to the greatest," declares the LORD. "For I will forgive their wickedness and will remember their sins no more."
>
> —JEREMIAH 31:33–34

> He said, "If you listen carefully to the voice of the LORD your God and do what is right in his eyes, if you pay attention to his commands and keep all his decrees, I will not bring on you any of the diseases I brought on the Egyptians, for I am the LORD, who heals you."
>
> —EXODUS 15:26

HEED MY CALL

—During a church service—

> In his hand is the life of every creature and the breath of all mankind.
>
> —JOB 12:10

Do not be deceived: God cannot be mocked. A

man reaps what he sows. The one who sows to please his sinful nature, from that nature will reap destruction; the one who sows to please the Spirit, from the Spirit will reap eternal life. Let us not become weary in doing good, for at the proper time we will reap a harvest if we do not give up.

—GALATIANS 6:7–9

My people have been lost sheep; their shepherds have led them astray and caused them to roam on the mountains. They wandered over mountain and hill and forgot their own resting place. Whoever found them devoured them; their enemies said, "We are not guilty, for they sinned against the LORD, their true pasture, the LORD, the hope of their fathers."

—JEREMIAH 50:6–7

Breathe deep, My children. Breathe deep. For as it is for your body, so it is for your spirit. For without thinking, without using your mind, yet your chest would expand; you would not see the air, yet it would fill you and there would be life, and it would sustain you. And so it is for My Spirit! That as you would humble yourself before Me, as you would bend to My will, as you would seek Me with your heart, so it is that My Spirit will fill you, and I will give you life, and I will sustain you. My Spirit, My children! My Spirit, My dear ones! For boldness. For your lives. That your life would be a testimony to Me and that I would use you to find My lost sheep, to find My children. For this is My desire. This is My heart. And, O that it would be your heart, that it would be your life, that you would take the cares and the lusts of this world and you would place them aside and you would place your eyes on Me; that you would place your eyes on things that are everlasting. Find My lost sheep! This is My call. My call to obedience—to you, My children. Remember these words. For they stand forever. This is your call, My children. This is your life. Remember these words.

> I am the good shepherd; I know my sheep and my sheep know me—just as the Father knows me and I know the Father—and I lay down my life for the sheep. I have other sheep that are not of this sheep pen. I must bring them also, they too will listen to my voice and there shall be one flock and one shepherd.
>
> —JOHN 10:14–16

> Heaven and earth will pass away, but my words will never pass away.
>
> —MATTHEW 24:35

SORROW UPON SORROWS

—During a church service to create support for missions—

> At that time they will see the Son of man coming in a cloud with power and great glory. When these things begin to take place, stand up and lift up your heads, because your redemption is drawing near.
>
> —LUKE 21:27–28

> Dear friends, now we are children of God, and what we will be has not yet been made known. But we know that when he appears, we shall be like him, for we shall see him as he is.
>
> —1 JOHN 3:2

> Then he will say to those on his left, "Depart
> from me, you who are cursed, into the eternal
> fire prepared for the devil and his angels."
>
> —MATTHEW 25:41

My children, you would hear of My second coming and you would think of what this would mean to you. How I would sweep you up into My arms to hold you, how you would see Me as I am, and how I would pour My love into you. You would see the joy and excitement of this day, but there is another side to this day, My children—sorrow upon sorrows. For think of yourselves as parents with your own child standing before you—and you love this child; your heart has not grown hard against him, and even now you want for nothing but to love this child and to have him love you. Even so, you must say to him, "Depart from Me. I will see you no more. Though you would call to Me I will never hear your voice again." Just as surely as I will come again, the day will come when this will happen for Me. For there are many of My children who do not know Me. There are many of My children who are lost. And though there is room in My heart for them, there will not be a place unless they know Me as Lord. This I speak to you in My own words that you would understand. And I would ask this of you, My children, that you would repent of your sins, that you would pray for the power of the Holy Spirit, and that you would do those things that I will place before you to do—for My Spirit will tell you what to do. Be it through your finances, or through your prayers, or through your works, I will show you what to do, and I will give you the strength to do it. With your obedience and the power of the Holy Spirit you will go out into this world where I will ask you to find My lost sheep, to find My lost children.

> The man without the Spirit does not accept the things that come from the Spirit of God, for they are foolishness to him, and he cannot understand them, because they are spiritually discerned.
>
> —1 CORINTHIANS 2:14

> Then Jesus told them this parable: "Suppose one of you has a hundred sheep and loses one of them. Does he not leave the ninety-nine in the open country and go after the lost sheep until he finds it? And when he finds it, he joyfully puts it on his shoulders and goes home. Then he calls his friends and neighbors together and says, 'Rejoice with me; I have found my lost sheep.' I tell you that in the same way there will be more rejoicing in heaven over one sinner who repents than over ninety-nine righteous persons who do not need to repent."
>
> —LUKE 15:3–7

MY HANDS

—During a church service—

> My command is this: Love each other as I have loved you. Greater love has no one than this, that he lay down his life for his friends.
>
> —JOHN 15:12–13

> Love is patient, love is kind. It does not envy, it does not boast, it is not proud. It is not rude, it is not self-seeking, it is not easily angered,

it keeps no record of wrongs. Love does not delight in evil but rejoices with the truth. It always protects, always trusts, always hopes, always perseveres.

—1 CORINTHIANS 13:4–7

While they were still talking about this, Jesus himself stood among them and said to them, "Peace be with you." They were startled and frightened, thinking they saw a ghost. He said to them, "Why are you troubled, and why do doubts rise in your minds? Look at my hands and my feet. It is I myself! Touch me and see; a ghost does not have flesh and bones, as you see I have."

—LUKE 24:36–39

My children! You would speak of love, and I stand before you now and I call you to Me. As you would come, I would lift My left hand and My right hand, and you would see the scars. You would see where the nails were driven through My hands for you. And I would say, be not appalled. Do not feel sorry, for this is My sign to you of My love, that My love is greater than My life; My love will last forever—and this is an enduring sign that you will know of My love. I would ask only that you would remember and that My love would pass through you. That you would love others as I love you, that you would bring them to Me, that you would find My lost children, that I might love them also. For My love is great. My love is bigger than you could know. My heart weeps for My children. I long for My children to come to Me. Bring them to Me. Bring Me My children, please!

This is love: not that we loved God, but that He

loved us and sent His Son as an atoning sacrifice for our sins.

—1 JOHN 4:10

For God so loved the world that He gave His
one and only Son, that whoever believes in him
shall not perish but have eternal life. For God
did not send His Son into the world to con-
demn the world, but to save the world through
him. Whoever believes in him is not condemned, but whoever does not believe stands
condemned already because he has not believed
in the name of God's one and only Son.

—JOHN 3:16–18

Or suppose a woman has ten silver coins and
loses one. Does she not light a lamp, sweep the
house and search carefully until she finds it?
And when she finds it, she calls her friends and
neighbors together and says, "Rejoice with me;
I have found my lost coin." In the same way, I
tell you, there is rejoicing in the presence of the
angels of God over one sinner who repents.

—LUKE 15:8–10

YOUR SHEPHERD

—During a prayer meeting—

The LORD is my shepherd, I shall not be in
want. He makes me lie down in green pastures,
he leads me beside quiet waters, he restores
my soul. He guides me in paths of righteousness for his name's sake. Even though I walk
through the valley of the shadow of death, I

will fear no evil, for you are with me; your rod
and your staff, they comfort me. You prepare a
table before me in the presence of my enemies.
You anoint my head with oil; my cup overflows.
Surely goodness and love will follow me all the
days of my life, and I will dwell in the house of
the LORD forever.

—PSALM 23

He tends his flock like a shepherd: He gathers
the lambs in his arms and carries them close
to his heart; he gently leads those that have
young.

—ISAIAH 40:11

My children! Do I not see you in this life? Do I not see
you as you would live your lives? And truly, My children,
I stand high above you, and I look into your heart, and
I see your lives; and to Me, My children, you are as My
sheep—you are the flock whom I watch over. And I would
see your lives—that you would scatter. I would see your
lives—that one would run wild in the hills, and yet another
would seek comfort by the stream, and others still would
watch their children in the meadow, and they would be
afraid of the wolf that would come—and they have lost
sight of the shepherd! For though I would look upon them,
yet they would not see, and they would not know. And
yet, My children, know My voice! And even as I speak, yet
they come to Me, and they gather around Me that I might
speak to them of My love, that I might hold them in My
arms, and that I would stand before them and protect
them. The confusion is gone. The peace would come, and
the prosperity; for it is My hand, My children—it is My
love; for I am the Good Shepherd—to you in your lives.

This is the time, My children, that the scattered sheep would come, that I would call and though they would not listen—yet even still I call and I call all the louder: I call them by name—for I know their names; I call them "My children," that they too would come. And this is My desire: that in each of your lives you would understand the desire of My heart. It is not for the miracles, My children, it is not that you would see the miraculous—it is that My sheep would come to Me. It is that as this life ends, yet the life continues and they would live it with Me for all of time and they would not be lost. They would not worry. There would be no fear and no pain. This is the desire of My heart—and, O that it would be the desire of your heart! O that every breath you take would be as a witness to Me. This is My desire, My children, and such is the time in which you live, such is the time that there would be faith, and I will honor the faith, for though you would not seek the miraculous—yet I am the God of the miraculous! Yet I cannot move without the miraculous! For every word I speak—it is so, My children! Every desire of My heart—it comes to pass, My children! This is My desire and this is as it shall be: I will call My children, they will hear, and they will come, and I will use you—as you are willing, as you would purify your hearts and live the life of the holy and righteous, as you would place My Word in your heart, then it will flow from your lips, My children. Even as the words flow from My lips, I will cause them to flow from your own. For this is My desire, this is My heart, and this is what shall be, My children.

> The man who enters by the gate is the shepherd
> of his sheep. The watchman opens the gate for

him, and the sheep listen to his voice. He calls his own sheep by name and leads them out. When he has brought out all his own, he goes on ahead of them, and his sheep follow him because they know his voice.

—JOHN 10:2–4

When he saw the crowds, he had compassion for them, because they were harassed and helpless, like sheep without a shepherd. Then he said to his disciples, "The harvest is plentiful but the workers are few. Ask the Lord of the harvest, therefore, to send out workers into his harvest field."

—MATTHEW 9:36–38

ABIDE IN ME

—During a church service—

For the earth will be filled with the knowledge of the glory of the LORD, as the waters cover the sea.

—HABAKKUK 2:14

O LORD, our Lord, how majestic is your name in all the earth! You have set your glory above the heavens.

—PSALM 8:1

Let them praise the name of the LORD, for his name alone is exalted; his splendor is above the earth and the heavens.

—PSALM 148:13

Do not worship any other god, for the LORD,

whose name is Jealous, is a jealous God.

—EXODUS 34:14

My children! My dear ones! As surely as the waters cover the sea and as surely as the earth is covered by the sky, yet My name covers all of creation. Yet My love covers all of My children—that you would know Me, that you would love Me. And so it is that I would speak to you now, My children—from My heart: that in every moment of every day yet a life would perish, and they would stand before Me and they would not know Me. And, O the despair of My heart. O the tears that I would cry. I am a jealous God, and I am jealous of your time, My children—your time away from Me. It is My desire that a new passion would be stirred within you, a new understanding of My character and My love, and a new zeal in your life for Me. As you meet—it is more than a service, it is more than a time of song and to hear the Word, yet it is a time when you will touch Me, and I will touch you. Draw near to Me, My children, for already I have drawn near to you. Abide in Me, My children, for already I abide in you and I live in you. I have breathed My Spirit within you that the passion, though it would be as a spark, yet I will fan the flames of the Spirit, My children, in a new way for you. This is My word, My children: that as surely as My love would cover you, yet My hand covers your heart, and I will give you a new heart as you will come to Me, as you will spend your time with Me, as you will follow after Me. It is the covering, My children, as surely as the sky would cover this earth, as surely as the waters cover the sea, look upon these things that they would be a sign that My love covers you, that My hand covers your heart.

Therefore, brothers, since we have confidence to enter the Most Holy Place by the blood of Jesus, by a new and living way opened for us through the curtain, that is, his body, and since we have a great priest over the house of God, let us draw near to God with a sincere heart in full assurance of faith, having our hearts sprinkled to cleanse us from a guilty conscience and having our bodies washed with pure water.

—HEBREWS 10:19–22

Remain in me, and I will remain in you. No branch can bear fruit by itself; it must remain in the vine. Neither can you bear fruit unless you remain in me.

—JOHN 15:4

The Light of Israel will become a fire, their Holy One a flame.

—ISAIAH 10:17

I will give you a new heart and put a new spirit in you; I will remove from you your heart of stone and give you a heart of flesh. And I will put my Spirit in you and move you to follow my decrees and be careful to keep my laws.

—EZEKIEL 36:26–27

I have put my words in your mouth and covered you with the shadow of my hand—I who set the heavens in place, who laid the foundations of the earth, and who say to Zion, "You are my people."

—ISAIAH 51:16

CONCLUSION

In our lives, there is nothing so awesome as the knowledge that there truly is a God, that He is the creator of all things, and that He is our own Father. There is nothing so wonderful as the love of Jesus who gave everything that was His to come and walk in this world so that we could have life and so that we could live in His love for all eternity. There is nothing in or of this world that in any way compares to the presence and the anointing the Lord pours into us through the Holy Spirit. There is nothing in this world for us—there is only the Lord who so freely gives, who so completely loves, and who so quickly speaks to us to draw us near to Him, to show us His unending love, and to provide direction, comfort, and encouragement for us as we live our lives. We may search for happiness and fulfillment in many different places and through many different ways, but there is only one who loves us and who is able to fill the emptiness within, and to heal every wound. There is only one true God. He is the Lord, and He is asking us to turn to Him, to love Him, and to live our lives for Him. He is our God, and He is asking us to rise up as individuals into the calling He has placed upon us, and as His church to fulfill His Great Commission He spoke upon us nearly two thousand years ago. Before we end, let's join together and offer this prayer to our awesome and loving God:

> Lord, I thank You for Your great love and that You have allowed me to know Your love. I know that I am not able to live without You, and I confess that although I have sinned in my life I am completely forgiven through the love and sacrifice of Jesus Christ. Jesus, I receive You in my heart right now, and I worship You in this moment, knowing that You are God and You are with me. Even now You know my thoughts; even now You know my needs; even now You are touching me and speaking into my heart so I will be encouraged and strengthened. Father, let my faith grow and my experience in You increase so I will have more of You—let me not feel complete unless I am in You. I ask now that You would help me to know Your ways, Your heart, and Your desires for me in my life. Let the Holy Spirit come upon me and enable me to be a bold witness for You. Give me a great passion for Your kingdom and for the lost. I pray now that my life would be as Jesus in the Garden, that I would surrender my will and my desires to You, and that I would drink in obedience the cup You have provided for me. Lord, let Your name be blessed in my life forever and ever. In Jesus' name I pray. Amen.

ABOUT THE AUTHOR

Over the last twenty years Mike has held positions in operations and supply chain management for semiconductor companies where he was responsible for buying, manufacturing, storing, and shipping products to satisfy customer demand. While working, Mike was actively involved with his local church where he taught children's Sunday school classes, assisted in adult Sunday school classes, hosted weekly prayer meetings in his home, and participated in prayer and deliverance ministry. In 1997 the Lord began to move in Mike's life in new and unexpected ways, and it is since that time that God has spoken prophetic words through him and has shown him things through the Holy Spirit that the Lord wants to share with His church. Recently, the Lord asked Mike and his wife, Janet, to relocate with their two children from their lifelong home in San Jose, California, to Franklin, Tennessee. Mike can be reached at:

P.O. Box 1453
Franklin, TN 37065
mike@mikeyrigoyen.com
www.mikeyrigoyen.com